ONE DAY
SELF GUIDED TOURS OF
SOUTHERN CALIFORNIA

TWENTY-SEVEN OUTLINED TOURS
WITH IDEAS AND INFORMATION FOR
MANY OTHER FUN-FILLED DAYS!

BEV GILLETT AND LAUREY VENN

**First Edition
B.B.L.T.
Irvine, California**

Published by B.B.L.T.
Irvine, California

First Edition
First Printing • 1,000 • October 1996

Library of Congress Catalog Card Number: 96-95119
ISBN 1-57502-359-8

Front and back covers designed by
Bev Gillett and Laurey Venn

Additional copies may be obtained by calling B.B.L.T. at
(714) 651-9822 or sending a fax to (714) 559-9041.
California State Tax and postage and handling will be added.

ONE DAY SELF GUIDED TOURS OF SOUTHERN CALIFORNIA
may be obtained by retail outlets at special rates. Write to the
above address for more information.

Printed in the USA by

*M*ORRIS
PUBLISHING

3212 E. Hwy 30
Kearney, NE 68847
800-650-7888

FORWARD

This book was born out of frustration! Frustration because there is so much to see and do in Southern California and surrounding areas, and frustration because one has to do hours worth of reading to get to "the bottom tourist line". We decided to simplify it all for you - and for any family or guests who may be visiting you - by offering self-guided, one day tours that are easy to follow, but above all, have the inside scoop only known to those who live, work and play here! We have omitted all of the extraneous tourist lures and gone right to the heart of what is - and what is not - the best to do and see in our beautiful area!

We hope you will put this book to good use. The print is large and easy to read, and the maps are simplified. We do, however, recommend that you invest in a Thomas Guide to keep in your car as the area is so large and can be confusing!

We have many people to thank of course, as the birth of a book of this kind is never without its labor coaches! Our wonderful husbands Bob and Tony for their unfailing support and a special thanks to Bob for hours of computer coaching and endless, patient help with all our questions. Our friends from the Newcomers Club of Irvine who helped us with editing - Ruth, Joan, Eileen, Maryette, Carol, Chris and Linda. Thanks also to Joyce for her advice and Carrie and Carolyn for proofreading. In addition, we had some professionals in the field who really gave us their all with no thought of recompense and to them we say a huge thank you! Georgiana and Larry Lester of Lester's Lithograph Inc., and "Uncle Harold" Haase of Career Publishing, Inc. Last but by no means least, our long-suffering children Cheryl and Brian (who laughed at us a lot but also helped with their computer knowledge!) and Lara, Andy and sister-in-law Wendy, who helped to brainstorm the title of the book!

Please join us now as we explore the magnificent Southern California that we love so much!

Bev. ___ Laurey

TABLE OF CONTENTS   <u>PAGE</u> <u>MAP</u>

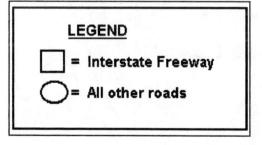

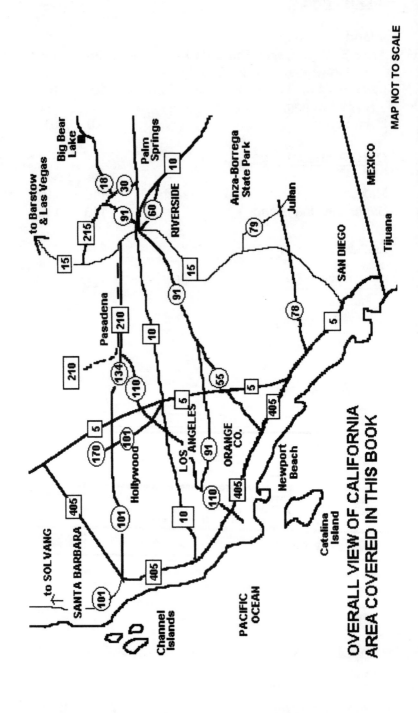

OVERALL VIEW OF CALIFORNIA
AREA COVERED IN THIS BOOK

MAP NOT TO SCALE

TO THE SOUTH - SAN DIEGO AREA

MAP NOT TO SCALE

CARLSBAD, LEUCADIA AND ENCINITAS
FLOWER CAPITAL OF SOUTHERN CALIFORNIA.

Too often we miss these three delightful coastal villages in our rush along the Interstate 5 on our way to or from San Diego. However, all three are beautiful and are becoming more well known as visitors discover some of the most spectacular flower displays anywhere in Southern California! Added to the flowers, you have some historic sites and also pristine, clear beaches! Bliss!

Carlsbad used to be called Agua Hedionda (Stinking Water) by the early soldiers because of the lagoon that was foul-smelling, but when a settler named **John Frazier** arrived in 1881 he discovered that the water was similar to the mineral water in the famous **Karlsbad Health Spa in Bohemia.** It became a favorite vacation spot for travelers and thus Carlsbad was born!

Also situated in Carlsbad is the well known, and high-priced **La Costa resort**, which has 36 holes of golf courses, a health spa and 23 tennis courts! (Call (800) 854-5000 to reserve accommodations.)

In the village itself are antique shops and some old Victorian homes well worth a visit.

The **flower fields** of Carlsbad bloom during May and June and can be seen behind **Andersen's Pea Soup Restaurant and Hotel** to the left of Interstate 5 going south. (This is easily identifiable by the huge windmill fronting the freeway!) These fields comprise millions of ranunculus, but also some more exotic bulbs from **South Africa** such as Sparaxis and Watsonia. They also have a colorful display of poinsettia in December. This is a definite must on your list of things to do and a wonderful photo opportunity to boot!

In the village on Elm Street, you will find **Rotary Park** and the old **Sante Fe train station**, which now serves as the **Visitors Bureau**.

Beyond the railroad tracks, turn right on Carlsbad Blvd., which is the main north-south street and go past Grand Avenue to reach the **Alt Karlsbad gift shop**, a replica of a Hanseatic house built on the site of John Frazier's well. They have an underground gallery depicting the old well and a mini-museum of Carlsbad history. They sell historical momentos and European handicrafts here.

Across the street and a block north on Beech Avenue you will find, in the park, the restored **Magee House**, which was built over a hundred years ago. It is now a museum of the **Carlsbad Historical Society**. The Magees' barn and carriage house as well as the first **St. Patrick's church** are here too. Close by on the corner of Grand and Roosevelt you will find an Irish pub called **Dooley McCluskey's**, which would be a good spot to have some lunch!

Now travel south on Carlsbad Blvd., also known as S21 to explore **Leucadia** and **Encinitas** with their wonderful flower nurseries and gardens, which are open to the public. The flowers grown here are a big business as they are shipped to florists all over America. Luckily the nurseries keep their own areas beautiful too and if you are visiting in Spring, do check out the thousands of ranunculus that grow in the **Frazee flower fields** opposite **South Carlsbad State Beach Park.**

Some of these wonderful nurseries are listed below, and we would advise you to wear comfortable clothing and walking shoes, especially if you are going to do some digging!

1. Stubbs Fuchsia Nursery, located at 737 Orpheus Ave, Leucadia.

They are open daily from 9 a.m.-5 p.m. and have over 30,000 flowering fuchsia plants, comprising more than 300 fuchsia varieties in every imaginable size, shape and color, along with a grand display of New Guinea impatiens. Many of these are in hanging baskets. (Tel: (619) 753-1069). They are closed on Tuesday.

2. Weidner's Begonia Gardens, located at 695 Normandy Road, Leucadia.

They are open 9:30 a.m.-5 p.m. from April 1-September 15, and again from November 1-December 22. They showcase 20,000 begonias in glorious colors and all in full bloom. The garden was established in 1973 when the Weidner family "retired" from the nursery business! You may wander around the rows to pick out your own plants and they will provide digging forks and instructions as well as carrying cartons for your plants. You may also bring your own pots and replant the begonias right there! These begonias are not expensive! There are other kinds of plants to purchase and view too such as fuchsias, impatiens and brunsfelsia.   The Weidners also have, in residence, assorted farmyard pets such as a pony, sheep, goat, ducks, pig and chickens!
(Tel. (619) 436-2194)

3. Quail Botanical Gardens, located at 230 Quail Gardens Drive, Encinitas.

This nature center comprises thirty acres of native, hybrid and imported plants and trees, as well as serving as a bird and wildlife sanctuary.   There are rangers living on the grounds who will be happy to answer any questions you may have, but they have five self-guided tours that are informative and easy to follow.

Our favorite trail is the **Quail Gardens Nature Trail** that will take you through chaparral plants to a pond planted with flora from all over California. It is important to be quiet in this area if you want to catch a glimpse of hummingbirds, doves and the California quail. You may also spot cottontail rabbit, long-tailed weasel, opossum, gray fox and pocket gophers.

The plants to be seen in this garden are really spectacular and unusual - many kinds of cactus, camphor trees, a bunya-bunya or monkey puzzle tree and also the Torrey pine, a tree that is now so rare that it is only seen in this area and on Santa Rosa Island.

The Quail Botanical Gardens are open daily from 9 a.m.-5 p.m. (and until 6 p.m. in summer). The entrance fee is $3 adults, children 5-12 years $1.50 and under 5, free. They have a gift shop and nursery on the premises too.
(Tel. (619) 436-3036)

4. Self-Realization Fellowship, located at 215 K Street, Encinitas.

This garden is a religious retreat situated on a cliff overlooking the ocean. It is easily visible by the golden-domed towers, which were built by sect members from India in the 1930's, and members now maintain a beautiful meditation garden inside the compound. The gardens are open daily from 9 a.m.-5 p.m. except Mondays. On Sundays they open from 9 a.m.-5 p.m. There is no charge to enter.
(Telephone: (714) 753-2888.)

As all three of these towns are close to the Interstate 5 they are easily accessible for all visitors.

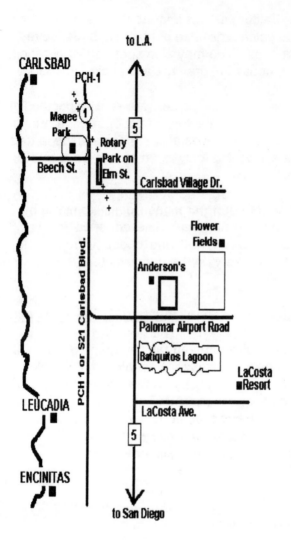

MAP NOT TO SCALE

FALLBROOK AND TEMECULA

Fallbrook is a rural village on the way to San Diego that is a delight to visit! You will feel as if you have stepped back into your childhood as you wander the countryside full of avocado and fruit trees, and spend time in the many stores.

Follow the signs to Fallbrook from Interstate 15 and wend your way amongst the orchards until you come to Mission Road, the downtown area filled with restaurants and antique stores! The village is full of unusual shops and quaint eateries, so stay a while and browse - you may come home with a treasure you never realized you needed! Do stop to buy some fresh fruit at one of the many roadside stands too. You could have lunch here at one of the delightful restaurants, but we would suggest that you wait to enjoy lunch at one of the wineries in Temecula.

After your sojourn in Fallbrook, head north on the Interstate 15 to the Rancho California Road exit that leads to **Temecula.** This is a burgeoning wine center and boasts nine wineries, with more on the way. All offer tours and tastings and interspersed amongst them you will find yet more antique shops!

Temecula got its start in the 1960's when Kaiser Aluminum Corp. acquired 90,000 acres of ranchland and began the planned community of **Rancho California**. The wineries begin four miles east of Temecula. You can do a circular wine tour by continuing east on Rancho California Road.

Some of the wineries you can visit are listed below and the ones with picnic facilities or a restaurant are starred:

The Hart Winery on the left hand side of the road. They have medal-winning Cabernet Sauvignon.

** **Callaway Winery** which is the biggest and best known of the local wineries and a must on your tour. They offer a wine tasting and have wine tours available. This is a good place to stop for a picnic lunch as they have tables shaded by a grape arbor.

** **John Culbertson Winery** is an impressive winery that also features a restaurant run by Martha Culbertson called **Cafe Champagne**, which is open 11 a.m. - 9 p.m. daily. This would be a super place to stop for lunch.

Piconi Winery is a small winery established by a Fallbrook doctor in 1981. The tasting room is open on weekends.

** **Mount Palomar** is the area's oldest winery. The entrance has a wooden wine cask on the road for easy identification. They make an excellent Riesling. They have a deli where you can buy food should you choose to picnic at a shaded table in the grounds.

Cilurzo Winery is a family run winery started in 1978 and they offer informal tours and tastings.

Britton Cellars is housed in a redwood and stained-glass building. They produce a good blush wine.

** **Maurice Carrie Winery** also sport a deli and picnic tables on the premises.

Filsinger Winery is known for its Chardonnay and Fume Blanc. Reach this winery by turning right from Rancho California Road onto Glenoaks Road before reaching Lake Skinner. Where this road dead-ends, turn right on DePortola Road and follow it to the winery.

Bailey Winery on Pauba Road is open on weekends only.

Return to Temecula by going right on DePortola Road and then left on Anza Road and right on California 79.

Additional Attractions in Temecula:

Hot-air balloon rides are becoming very popular and there are three companies that offer tours. All celebrate the 45 to 90 minute flights with the traditional toast of champagne. In May they celebrate the annual **Rancho California Balloon and Wine Festival**. Call the Temecula Chamber of Commerce at (909) 676-5090 for details.

The Wild Animal Park is located to the East of this area. This would be a full day excursion on its own. Follow the I-15 to Hwy. 78 East and continue onto the Park. This park offers a full day's touring as well as overnight camping spots in their grounds - good fun for the kids! Call for reservations - (619) 747-8702.

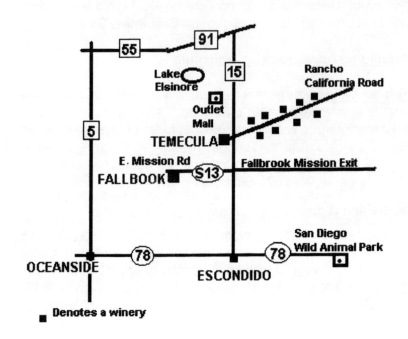

MAP NOT TO SCALE

JULIAN

We have many delightful villages in Southern California, but none so quaint as **Julian**, nestled in the foothills of the Cleveland National Forest and now sporting the title of the Apple Capital of California. Visiting Julian is like taking a giant step back in time to an easier, kinder lifestyle, so join us and take the tour!

You will follow the I-5 Fwy. south to Oceanside and then take Hwy. 78 East through San Marcos. Continue on this road (follow it carefully as it meanders through small villages) en route to **Ramona.** (The yearly play they stage there about the early Indians calls for hundreds of locals to become actors and is quite a famous event!)

Continuing on Hwy 78. you will come to **Santa Ysabel**, home of the fabled **Dudley's Bakery.** This is a great bread shop that sells about twenty-one different kinds of breads, not to mention cookies and rolls, but be warned, they sell out quite early in the morning, so you run the risk of being disappointed if you plan to stop here on your return trip! Follow your nose around the corner to the **Pie Shop** and stop to watch the apples being cored and made into pies before your eyes! Of course, a slice of apple pie a la mode with a glass of apple cider will hit the spot! If time permits, there is an **Indian Mission** here that you could tour. (See 2. at the end of the tour).

Turn right on Hwy. 79 and follow the signs to Julian, and once in the village, park your car as this is a place best explored on foot! The town was created when miners rushed here to stake claims in 1870 during a gold strike.

There are many Hotels and Bed and Breakfasts, at least one of which dates from that period.

The Pine Hills Lodge has a barbecue dinner theater starring local performers every Saturday evening.

As you meander around the village, which is only about eight blocks square, you will find many country and antique stores and everywhere pie shops, restaurants and other homage to apples in all their various forms! Have lunch somewhere - more pie - yummy!

Be sure to visit the **Julian Memorial Museum** at Washington and Fourth Streets, which is full of nostalgia from the past century. This building was a former brewery. On the hill behind the Museum you will find the town library as well as a one-room schoolhouse that was built in 1888 and moved from nearby Witch Creek. You will also come across the **Julian Drug Store**, built in 1886, where you can enjoy a drink at the old marble-topped fountain.

Up the hill on C. Street is the **Eagle Mine**, where you can learn about Julian's past and the gold rush days. They have a tour that goes 1,000 feet into the tunnels that will give you a good insight into the early days!

There are many horse-drawn carriages and wagons in the village adding to the Victorian atmosphere.

Note: Julian can be chilly at best or downright cold in Winter, so be sure to take a sweater .. just in case! Please be aware of the fact that they sometimes experience icy conditions so tire chains may be required. These can be rented en route if necessary.

Julian is a splendid place for a weekend visit too, as there is so much to do in the surrounding area!
Other Places of Interest:

1. **Cuyamaca Rancho State Park**:

This park is located about ten miles south of Julian on California 79.

Follow signs that lead to **Stonewall Mine**, which you will find near the entrance to **Paso Picacho** campground. There is an Interpretive Center located here which will tell you all about the local fauna and flora.   For wonderful views, we recommend the three-mile trail to **Cuyamaca Peak**, from where, on a clear day, you can see the desert, the ocean and Mexico! You can call (619) 765-0755 to make camp reservations, up to six months prior to your desired date. The fee to make a reservation is $6.75. They have many campgrounds here, including places where you may take your horses and dogs!

2. **Mission Santa Ysabel**.

This mission is located in **Santa Ysabel** (near Dudley's Bakery) and was founded in 1818 as an assistencia (Branch) of the mother mission in San Diego.   They welcome visitors to the church and the museum. It continues to serve local Indians from ten reservations. Points of interest include the religious murals painted by the Indians and the Indian burial grounds.

3. **Lake Henshaw and Palomar Observatory**.

Continue north and turn west on California 76 towards **Lake Henshaw**. This is a very popular local fishing spot! Follow San Diego County Road 57, East Grade Road to the summit road junction on **Palomar Mountain**.   Then go right on S6, the **Highway to the Stars**, to the **Palomar Observatory**. This route will take you through some spectacular mountain and forest scenery, but be warned that in winter they experience heavy snowfalls and snow chains may be required.An immense white dome (twelve stories high) houses the 200-inch **Hale telescope**, America's largest, and you may view this instrument from a gallery.   The telescope is only used by scientists at night, who take photographs and and electronic images of the stars and beyond. It has a huge mirror made of Pyrex glass, which took eleven years to grind and polish to perfection. However, scientists can now see as far as a sextillion miles into space! Pamphlets in the area also tell of other feats of the telescope. The observatory is open from 9 a.m.-4 p.m. and is free. Call (619) 742-2119.

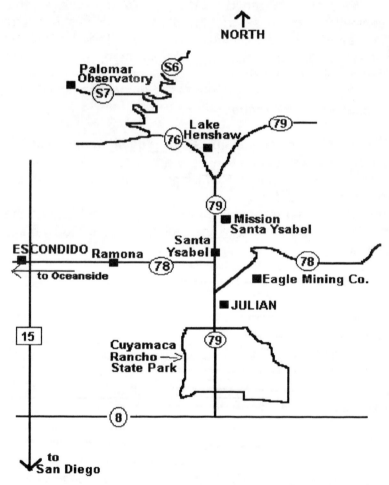

MAP NOT TO SCALE

LA JOLLA AND DEL MAR

La Jolla is one of the most exclusive suburbs of San Diego and with good reason - miles and miles of pristine beaches, a plethora of shops, art galleries and restaurants and plenty of parks for picnics, make it a must-see for a day trip! Add to that a fantastic coastline filled with caves, marine life and stunning views - how could it miss!

Drive south along I-5 to the La Jolla Village Drive exit. Head west along the rim of the **UCSD campus** and turn left on Torrey Pines Road. Then go right on Prospect Place, and then sharp right on Coast Blvd. Coast Blvd. is a steep street heading straight down to the ocean. Find parking outside the **Shell Shop** on your right hand side and take a walk along the cliff tops, enjoying the outstanding views. You may also view the **La Jolla Cave** after descending a set of 140 stairs located inside the Shell Shop - there is a nominal charge for entry. This ten-story tunnel takes you down to one of the caves from where you can get a bird's eye view of the sandstone cliffs of La Jolla. (Warning: It is an easy walk going down, but can be "aerobically challenging" coming back up! There is a stair rail to help you.)

We recommend that you continue your walk along Coast Blvd. until you reach the park, passing **Bird Rock** where you are guaranteed a view of all sorts of coastal birds, including the California brown pelicans, and maybe a seal or two!

Return for your car at this point, as you will continue along Coast Drive until you come to a large Lifeguard Station, at the Children's Pool, perched atop the cliffs from where you can walk out into the ocean on a specially constructed board walk to view the **sea lions** on the beach. This is a must and a great photo opportunity!

Now - time for shopping as you return to Prospect Street to take in the wonderful variety available to tempt your pocketbook!   Do stop in at another famous landmark, the 1926 **Hotel La Valencia**, easily recognizable because of its pink tower with a gilded top.

The views overlooking the ocean are outstanding from their patio dining area, and this would be one of many good spots for lunch!

The next stop on your trip is **Del Mar**. Turn left from Prospect Place onto Torrey Pines Road, and then follow it up the hill turning left onto North Torrey Pines Road. This will skirt the campus of UCSD. Drive north to Torrey Pines Scenic Drive, beyond the **Salk Institute for Biological Studies**, and then turn left and go to the end of the road at the cliff top. This is a small detour in order to view the dramatic scenery along the coastal cliff top, and the spot from where hang gliders take off and radio-controlled model airplanes are launched!

Return to North Torrey Pines Road and continue north, until the road descends to the ocean. This road is San Diego County S21, which becomes Camino Del Mar and brings you into the heart of the coastal village of **Del Mar**. This too is loaded with quaint shops and eateries, and of course Del Mar is most famous for its national horse show, the **Del Mar Fair** and finally its thoroughbred racing season, which takes place at the **Del Mar Race Track**.

Horses apart, the scenery and beaches are divine and the laid back atmosphere in Del Mar makes for a very pleasant visit! There are a couple of restaurants located right on the beach here - **Jake's** and **Poseidon,** both of which offer splendid views of the ocean.

Other Places of Interest for another day!

1. **Torrey Pines State Reserve** - the only State park where you may not picnic, smoke or even have a dog in the car!

This reserve is home to a very rare tree, the Torrey pine, which is only found in two places in the world and is a relic of the Ice Age. This park is a 1,000 acre reserve and offers a variety of foot trails. It is located on North Torrey Pines Road. Entrance is $4 per car, walkers and cyclists are free. Guided nature walks on weekends at 11:30 a.m. and 1:30 p.m. (Bicycles are not allowed on the trails).

2. **Birch Aquarium at Scripps,** part of the **Oceanographic Institute**, a graduate division of UCSD, is located on the bluff tops of La Jolla. There is a man-made tide pool where you can view and photograph nearly two dozen live marine creatures, while inside are eighteen large tanks that show ocean habitats along the coastline of Southern California as well as Baja, Mexico.

To reach the aquarium from La Jolla, turn left from Prospect Place onto North Torrey Pines Road. The aquarium is well signboarded. Visitors can watch fish being fed on Sunday and Wednesday afternoons at 1:30 p.m. Entrance is $6.50 for adults, $5.50 for seniors, $4.50 for students and $3.50 for children 3-12 years. Those under 3 are free. Parking is $3 per car. Call (619) 534-3474 for more information.

3. **Knorr Candle Factory,** 14906 Via de la Valle, Del Mar. This candle factory, owned and operated by the same family since the 1920's, is well worth a visit! It boasts a huge showroom that is open seven days a week from 9 a.m.-5 p.m. There is a factory on the property which should be open by April 1997 for tours. In addition, they sell beekeeping and candlemaking supplies. The candles that appealed to us included scented candles, "garden" candles made with citronella, animal shaped candles and anniversary and Unity candles (which you may order for your specific event). There is an enormous Christmas display which begins at the end of October. Upstairs is "Judy's Attic", full of Southwestern candles! It is all surrounded by a pretty garden!

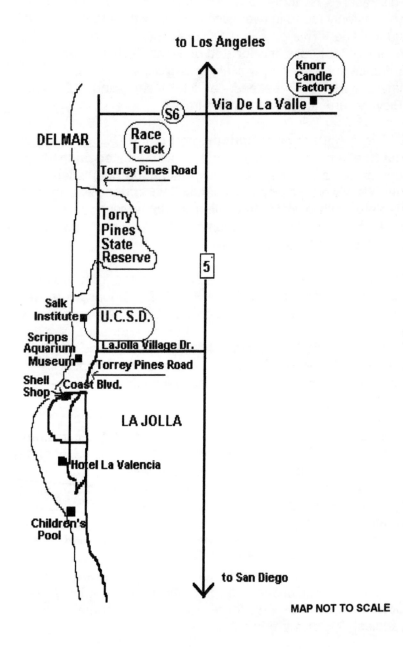

to Los Angeles

Knorr Candle Factory

S6 Via De La Valle

DELMAR

Race Track

Torrey Pines Road

Torry Pines State Reserve

5

Salk Institute

U.C.S.D.

Scripps Aquarium Museum

LaJolla Village Dr.

Torrey Pines Road

Shell Shop

Coast Blvd.

LA JOLLA

Hotel La Valencia

Children's Pool

to San Diego

MAP NOT TO SCALE

SAN DIEGO

In 1769 Don Gaspar de Portola established the first Spanish fort and Father Junipero Serra built the first Franciscan mission, making San Diego the birthplace of California and, in our opinion, one of the jewels of the California coast!

Follow the I-5 Fwy south to San Diego and exit at **Old Town Historic Park**. Adobe and log structures reflect the Mexican Colonial architecture of the area as it was in the mid-1800's. This is a colorful shopping area called **Bazaar del Mundo**, and it is set in a six block state historic park. Intermingled with shops and restaurants are a dozen vintage buildings that are fun to tour and show life as it was during the days of the early settlers. Park rangers offer free walking tours of the area each afternoon, or you can pick up a free guide map from any of the merchants and tour on your own.

Before you get lost in the shops, remember to book your **Old Town Trolley Tour**, which we highly recommend if this is your first trip to the area. The tour costs $20 for adults, $8 for children 6-12 years old and is free to anyone younger than 6. The tour they offer is comprehensive and you may get on and off the trolley at any of their many stops throughout the San Diego area without worrying about parking for your car! This tour includes:

Balboa Park, the city's cultural center - lots of museums, art galleries, theaters, the famous **San Diego Zoo** and beautiful gardens.

Seaport Village, a quaint shopping area with a boardwalk on the ocean - lots of shops and restaurants and usually a wandering entertainer or two!

Horton Plaza, a pretty outdoor shopping mall in the center of San Diego. This area also includes the **Gaslamp Quarter**, which was an area of ill repute in days gone by, now restored to quaint Victoriana and abounding with shops and eateries. It is a designated Historic District.

Coronado Island and the beautiful, historic **Hotel del Coronado**, where the Prince of Wales reportedly met Wallace Simpson and where many Presidents and famous people come to stay. The other side of the small island is where you will find the site of the America's Cup yacht races, and also where you can catch the ferry back to Seaport Village or take a tour of the harbor. (If you have a few hours on Coronado Island, rent a bicycle and tour the island that way! It is small enough to do easily in an hour or two!)

The above tours will be a full day of touring, especially if you get on and off the trolley to explore as you should do! The guides are informative and will give you a comprehensive oversight to the history of the City.

Should you wish to visit San Diego for a weekend, we would suggest you find yourself a reasonably priced hotel on the Hotel Circle (near the exit to Old Town on Hwy. 8). San Diego is full of interesting places to explore, and here are a few more definitely worth seeing:

Cabrillo National Monument - a good spot for nature lovers - super views and whale watching in season. Entrance is $2 for pedestrians and cyclists and $4 per car. It is open from 9 a.m. to dusk.

The Wild Animal Park - located about 30 miles north of San Diego on Hwy. 78. You can call to reserve an overnight camping spot in their grounds - good fun for the kids! Entrance is $18.95 for adults, Seniors over 60, $17.05, and children 3-11 years $11.95. Parking is $3. They are open from 9 a.m.-4 p.m. Telephone: (619) 747-8702.

Sea World - definitely a full day in and of itself! (On Sea World Drive off I-5. See map.) Admission costs $30.95 for adults, $22.95 for children and $23.75 for seniors over 55 years. Parking: cars $5, R.V.'s $7. Open 9 a.m. with varying closing times. Telephone: (619) 222-6363.

Mission Bay - 4,800 acres of water and park! Rent a sailboat, ride a gondola and definitely go and see the Crystal Pier. (Off I-5 - visible from the freeway).

The Palomar Observatory near the town of Julian. (See map of Julian area.)

San Diego Bay and Embarcadero where you can do a harbor cruise and see the tuna fishing fleets at work.

Tijuana - over the border into **Mexico**. You can take the red trolleys from near Horton Plaza or drive yourself down to the border, park your car and walk over the bridge. Take a cab to Avenue Revolucion. **Remember** - you will need a photo ID such as a driver's license, or a passport (if you are not a US citizen) to exit Mexico. (See the Tijuana tour in this book.)

Wineries nearby in Escondido and Temecula.

La Jolla. This deserves a special page all by itself as it is so beautiful, but be sure to explore it a little. It is north of San Diego and the home of University of California, San Diego. (See page 21 for complete La Jolla tour!)

All the above places are worthy of a day's excursion, but we would recommend the Old Town Trolley Tour as the best overview of the area, keeping note of which places to enjoy on your return trip!

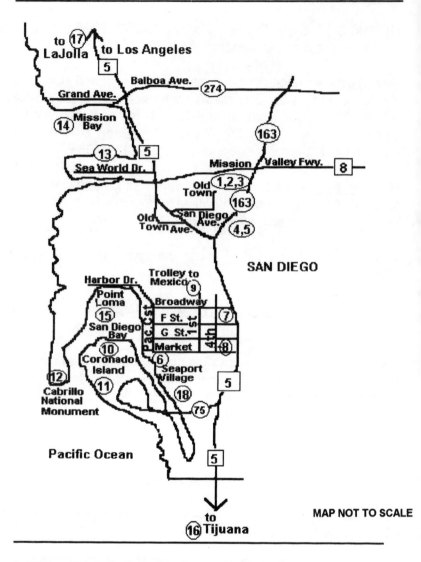

to (17) LaJolla   to Los Angeles
5
Balboa Ave.   (274)
Grand Ave.
(14) Mission Bay
163
(13)
Sea World Dr.   Mission   Valley Fwy.   8
Old Town   (1,2,3)
163
Old Town Ave.   San Diego Ave.   (4,5)
SAN DIEGO
Trolley to Mexico (9)
Harbor Dr.
Point Loma   Broadway
(15)   F St.   7
San Diego Bay   G St.
(10)   Market   8
Coronado Island   (6)
(12)   (11)   Seaport Village
Cabrillo National Monument   (18)   5
75
Pacific Ocean   5

to (16) Tijuana

MAP NOT TO SCALE

1. Old Town Historic Pk
2. Bazaar del Mundo
3. Old Town Trolley
4. Balboa Park
5. San Diego Zoo
6. Seaport Village
7. Horton Plaza

8. Gaslamp Quarter
9. Trolley to Mexico
10. Coronado Island
11. Hotel Coronado
12. Cabrillo National
     Monument
13. Sea World

14. Mission Bay
15. San Diego Bay
16. Tijuana
17. La Jolla
18. Convention Ctr.

IN THE MIDDLE: ORANGE COUNTY

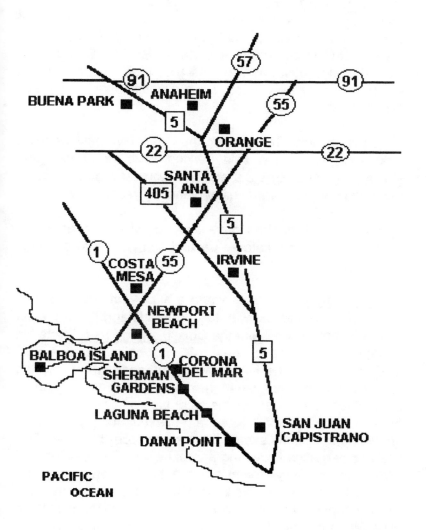

MAP NOT TO SCALE

NEWPORT BEACH, BALBOA ISLAND, CORONA DEL MAR, SHERMAN GARDENS AND FASHION ISLAND

Newport Beach has miles of beautiful, sandy beaches, charming beach homes and colorful gardens. It is a must-see and the logical place to start your trip today! Follow the 55 Fwy. south, which becomes Newport Blvd. until you cross PCH (Pacific Coast Highway). As you cross the highway you will see some of the fabulous yachts that jam-pack this area - 10,000 in all!

Take the first left after crossing the Coast Overpass onto Via Lido and park in the paid parking structure at the **Lido Marina Village**. This is a pretty spot with cozy, outdoor cafes perched beside a marina full of gleaming yachts!

Newport Pier is a short drive away on West Ocean Front. Find yourself some metered parking and get set to do some exploring!

The Newport Pier itself is worth a stroll - lots of fishermen and super views all the way to **Catalina Island** if it is a clear day! Be sure to check out the **Dory Fishing Fleet.** Started in 1889, this fleet is the last beachside fishing cooperative of its kind in the U.S. The fishermen go out early in the morning and return to sell their fish to their local customers from about 9 a.m. Stroll past some of the local bars and shops for a bit of added local color. Keep an eye out for parrots atop shoulders and many skateboarders and roller bladers! This is a popular place for young and old alike! The walking and cycling trail extends for miles in both directions along the front of the homes in this area. Continue on Newport Blvd. which changes its name to Balboa Blvd. and turn right on Main Street to reach the **Balboa Pier**. (There is a tiny **Ruby's Diner** at the end of the pier!).

It is easiest to park in the public parking here and then wander through the little village, stopping for a coffee, soda or ice cream at one of the quaint eateries.

Make your way towards the **Balboa Pavilion** (a Victorian structure that was once a bath house and a terminal for the Pacific Electric Red Car Line). You will find the **Catalina Passenger Service** here which operates tours to Catalina Island as well as narrated cruises of **Newport Harbor**. Highly recommended is the 45 minute tour within the harbor, so you can ooh and aah at all the beautiful homes and yachts in the area! (Cost $6 adults, $1 children 5-12 years). There are seven islands making up the Harbor - not all visible from the road, so this boat cruise is a must! They also have a 90 minute tour, which goes to the open ocean area.

If deepsea fishing is to your liking, you will find **Newport Landing Sportfishing** on 400 Main St. They offer fishing trips of varying lengths, and charge $6.30 for a one-day license. Call (714) 675-0550 for times of departure.

Continue the tour in your car, following signs to the **Balboa Bay Ferry,** which is also located near the Balboa Pavilion next to the giant Ferris wheel, and take the ferry across to **Balboa Island.** (This costs $1 per car, including driver, 35c for each adult and 15c for a child). This island is composed of two parts, but the main section is only a couple of miles around and makes for a terrific walk.   In December the homes are beautifully decorated, as are all the fabulous yachts and docks! There are super eateries in the main street (Marine Drive) which are well worth a stop for lunch! It is reminiscent of an English village!

Follow Marine Avenue north and cross the bridge leaving the island until you once again come to PCH. Turn right and follow PCH until you come to **Corona Del Mar**. There is a magnificent two-acre garden called **Sherman Gardens** on the right hand side (in the middle of the village) that is definitely worth a visit. Their landscaped gardens house more than 2,000 plant species. You may enter for a nominal fee. They also have a tea garden and a very good gift shop. After you have seen Sherman Gardens, turn right on Marguerite and travel to the ocean front for some spectacular views from the headlands of **Corona del Mar** as well as Newport and Balboa. This is a good photo opportunity! Walk along the headlands to look down on the main swimming beach and enjoy all the scenery.

Retrace your route along PCH and turn right into **Fashion Island** where you may finish off your lovely day. This is a glitzy market place, featuring streets lined with quaint boutiques and specialty stores as well as all the large department stores. The streets and plazas are filled with pull-carts selling all manner of goods. The center has many fine dining establishments as well as a Farmer's Market downstairs featuring all kinds of food to carry out or eat in and even features a piano player! Across the road is the Hard Rock Cafe - easy to find as they have a 40' electric guitar pointing to the entrance! Another fun spot is the Cheesecake Factory, where you can sit at the bar counter and oversee the whole ocean front.

Additional Notes:
I. Every Christmas, this area has a **Christmas Boat Parade** between Dec. 17 - 23. You may buy a ticket to be a passenger on a boat or watch from the shore. We have found an excellent vantage point to be on Balboa Island and we enjoy strolling around looking at the beautifully lit and decorated homes in this area before the parade begins!

2.   **Rogers Gardens** is located on MacArthur Blvd. near Fashion Island, and is also a must-see at Christmas time with an incredible display of decorated Christmas trees, ornaments and gardens. This is a must even for the non-gardeners amongst you!

3.   The **Marriott Hotel** located near Fashion Island offers spectacular views from the View Lounge on the 16th floor of the North Tower. This is especially good at twilight or in the evening to catch all the lights of the surrounding area.

4.   The **Four Seasons Hotel** on Newport Center Drive is located along the same drive that circles Fashion Island and features a top-notch afternoon tea!   This hotel is where President George Bush used to stay when he visited Orange County. Needless to say, the prices are high.

5.   The **Upper Newport Bay State Ecological Reserve**, fondly referred to as "The Back Bay" by the locals, is a wonderful spot to enjoy walking, cycling, hiking, canoeing or kayaking. The best time to visit, if you are a bird-lover, is November when migrating bird populations are at their peak, but you will see all kinds of birds and waterfowl year round. To reach this area take Pacific Coast Highway to Jamboree Road, turn left on Back Bay Drive and you will run right into the Bay! There is no charge to enter here.
The nearby **Newport Dunes RV Park** is located near PCH and they have sailboats, paddleboats and kayaks available for use on their 15-acre lagoon. They offer more than 400 RV spaces and a large boat launching area. There is an eatery called "**The Back Bay Cafe**" located in the parking lot of the Newport Dunes RV Park, which we highly recommend. Call (714) 640-1751 for information on "The Back Bay" and (714) 729-3863 for Newport Dunes RV Park information.

1. Dory Fisherman
2. Newport Pier
3. Catalina Island
4. Balboa Pavilion
5. Balboa Pier

MAP NOT TO SCALE

THE ANAHEIM AND BUENA PARK AMUSEMENT AREAS

We are going to explore the less obvious tourist features of these two cities today, as we are sure you have "done" both **Disneyland** in **Anaheim** and **Knott's Berry Farm** in **Buena Park**! If you haven't, it goes without saying that they should both be featured at the top of your "to do" list in these areas. They will each take a full day on their own!

We find the most activities centered in Buena Park close to Knotts Berry Farm, so we will start there and list all the activities available!

I. **Movieland Wax Museum located at 7711 Beach Blvd.**
Featured here are more than 240 movie and TV stars re-created in Hollywood sets - all in wax of course!
Open daily at 9 a.m. Adults $9.95, children 4-11 years $5.95.

2. **Hobby City is located further up the road at 1238 Beach Blvd.**
This is a fascinating place to visit as they have a privately run museum and also a group of craft and collector shops all set within the center, where you can indulge all your fancies and pick up some valuable crafting supplies while you are visiting. We love the cake decorating shop and the bear shop set in a replica of a tree!

Inside the **Doll and Toy Museum** (housed in a half-scale replica of the White House) you can admire more than 2,000 rare, antique dolls and toys from all over the world. This is open daily from 10 a.m.- 6 p.m. and costs $1 for adults and 50 cents for children under 12 years.

Apart from the many shops there is an area especially built for the small fry, where a miniature train huffs and puffs around its tracks. It is a most popular venue for birthday parties for the younger set.

3. Medieval Times located at 7662 Beach Blvd.

Medieval Times recreates a spectacle of the Middle Ages with knights jousting on horseback during your four-course dinner. Audience participation in all the fun and hilarity is required! Admission includes the tournament and a meal with two rounds of drinks. Price is $28 for adults on Fridays and Saturdays, $26 for other evenings, $24 for weekend matinees. Children cost $18 in the evenings, $16 for a matinee. Call (714) 521-4740 to make a reservation.

Anaheim offers a few surprises too, namely:

1. **The Disneyland Hotel** located opposite the Park, is a full-fledged resort with a man-made marina complete with **pedal boats** and a sandy beach. In addition, the 60-acre garden sports three swimming pools. There is also a shopping bazaar called **Seaports of the Pacific** bordering the marina, and twice nightly there is a show of **dancing waters,** colored lights and music to entertain hotel guests. They also have remote-controlled **miniature boats** in the marina and **small cars** racing around an off-road raceway!

There is no charge to enjoy any of this as it is attached to the hotel, but you would have to pay the parking fee to park in the grounds. The hotel features many restaurants, and is a fun place to visit in addition to Disneyland itself!

2.   **Anaheim Convention Center** on 800 West Katella Avenue offers concerts, as well as all kinds of shows and conventions each week. Watch your newspaper for current events.

3. **Anaheim Stadium**, or the "Big 'A'" is at 2000 South State College Blvd. and offers baseball games mid-April through September. It is the home of the **California Angels baseball team**.   Call (714) 634-2000 for schedule and ticket information. It also hosts the bigger conventions and shows such as the **Recreational Vehicle Shows.**

4. **The Anaheim Pond** is very close to the Anaheim
Stadium, and is the home of the of **Disneyland Mighty
Ducks of Anaheim Ice Hockey Team**.   Watch your
newspaper for forthcoming show attractions as well as Ice
Hockey games.

COSTA MESA, SANTA ANA AND IRVINE
"SHOPPING, THEATER, ART AND BUSINESS"

The heart of Orange County, comprised of these three cities, has enjoyed tremendous growth in recent years. You will find high-rises with sleek, glass facades encroaching on strawberry fields, as well as suburban sprawl in all directions. Many high-powered, world-class businesses have made this area their headquarters, as have smaller companies.

South Coast Plaza, in Costa Mesa, is an elegant shopping "city" that has been designated an official tourist attraction by the State of California. You can find this area along the 405 Fwy. exiting at Bristol. If your hotel is located in Anaheim, the Pacific Coast Greyline motor coach offers a round trip to South Coast Plaza for $8. (Call 978-8855).

South Coast Plaza is home to almost every major retailer in the world, from upscale department stores such as Macy's, Robinsons-May, Nordstroms and Saks Fifth Avenue to many designer names such as Charles Jourdan, Giorgio Armani and Versace. The interior is sleek and polished and sports marble walkways and dazzling fountains.

Across the street is the second part of South Coast Plaza, named **Crystal Court**. You will find more designer names here such as Alfred Sung, Esprit, Galleri Orrefors Kosta Boda alongside boutiques and department stores such as Robinsons-May. The Crystal Court hosts a magnificent **Orchid Show** once a year when the walkways and interior are transformed with bowers of flowers. It is easy to get from Crystal Court to South Coast Plaza - use the courtesy bus or simply walk across.

Leaving South Coast Plaza, cross the pedestrian bridge called Unity Bridge at the east end of the Plaza to reach **Town Center**. This area is the mecca of performing arts for the area, and also home to many premier restaurants representing food from around the world!

Some of the works of art in the area are located in a 1.6-acre garden called **California Scenario Park**. This park, filled with oversized sculptures, is located between the Great Western Bank and Comerica towers off Anton Blvd. The most famous piece, **California Scenario by Japanese-American sculptor Isamu Noguchi** is definitely worth a visit as are other pieces by **Carl Milles, Joan Miro, Henry Moore and Charles Perry** located further down the walkways. The sculptures are made of natural materials such as rocks, sand and water.

The **Orange County Performing Arts Center** is the County's pride and joy! You will find music and dance of all kinds presented here as well as the Pacific Symphony Orchestra and Opera Pacific and Pacific Chorale. The main stage, Segerstrom Hall, has a remarkable sculpture called **Fire Bird, created by Richard Lippold**, which has become a recognized symbol of Orange County. This sculpture is made of silver, red and gold aluminum and is integrated into both the interior lobby spaces and exterior Grand Portal area, signifying the eternal spirit of the arts ascending. (For ticket information, call 957-4033)

Returning to the 405 Fwy. travel south to Irvine, to locate the **Irvine Museum** on Von Karman Avenue. (Information 476-0294). The museum is in a temporary location of an Irvine office building - Tower 17, Douglas Plaza. There is no admission fee. (Look for the American flag on top of the round building!)

The paintings in this museum are from the collection of Joan Irvine Smith, who has more than 2,000 such paintings. Most of these works date from between 1890-1930 and depict California land and seascapes. These were artists who belonged to the school of "California Impressionists". They include notable works by painters such as **Granville Redmond, William Wendt and Guy Rose**.

Also in Irvine is to be found the **Irvine Barclay Theater**, located on the campus of the University of California, Irvine. This theater showcases musical, dramatic and dance events. (Call 854-4646 for information).

The Bowers Museum of Cultural Art at 2002 N. Main St. in Santa Ana is Orange County's largest museum. The collection reflects the predominant cultures that shaped early California - the local Native American Indian tribes as well as the Spanish and Mexican influences from the 1700s until 1850, when California became a state. Also to be found are artifacts from many Pacific Rim cultures. The building, a re-creation of a Spanish mission is impressive and has a fine restaurant, The Topaz Cafe, on the property too. (Take the I-5 Fwy to 17th Street, turn right and then make another right at Main Street. Entrance fee is $6 adults, children 5-12 $2, seniors over 62 $4 and students with I.D. $4. Tel: (714) 567-3600.

Other Points of Cultural Interest:

I. Although located in the city of Garden Grove, the **Crystal Cathedral** is a must see! This cathedral is the home of Dr. Robert Schuller, and it got its start as a drive-in church! It is now a towering twelve-story edifice of glass surrounded by magnificent gardens and impressive statutory. It is the home of **The Hour of Power** television show.

Regardless of your religious persuasion, this cathedral is a must-see. The Crystal Cathedral stages two Biblical spectacles during the year, at Easter and at Christmas.

Directions: Take the Chapman Ave. exit off the Santa Ana Fwy. (I-5) and head west for a few blocks to Lewis Street. Tours are offered daily. (Call 971-4000 for information).

2. **Discovery Museum of Orange County**. This lies a few miles southwest of Bowers Museum at 3101 W. Harvard. The 1898 Kellogg House is a journey into a Victorian era and a good place to bring the youngsters as they can dress in authentic clothing, churn their own butter and watch a blacksmith ply his trade. You can visit the house, the carriage house and the water tower. Hours of operation are 1-5 p.m. on Wed., Thurs. and Fri. and 11 a.m.-3 p.m. on Sunday. Entrance fee is $3.50 for adults and $2.50 for seniors and children. Telephone: (714) 540-0404.

3. **The Howe-Waffle House** at 120 Civic Center Dr. West was built in 1889 by Orange County's first female doctor, Wilella Howe-Waffle and her husband. This house is well preserved and sports stained glass windows, panelled walls and eight foot "pocket" doors that slide in and out of walls. The house is open on the second Tuesday of every month between 10 a.m.-2 p.m. and on the second Sunday of every month between 1-4 p.m. There is a $3 donation requested. You may reserve a special time to view the house if you have a party by calling (714) 543-8282.

4. **The Santa Ana Zoo**, located off Fwy I-5 at First Street in Prentice Park, showcases 250 different species. There is a special exhibit on primates as well as an aviary and a children's zoo. The entrance fee is $3.50 for ages 13-59, $1.50 for ages 3-12 and seniors over 60 years, and free for children under 2 years. Telephone: (714) 836-4000.

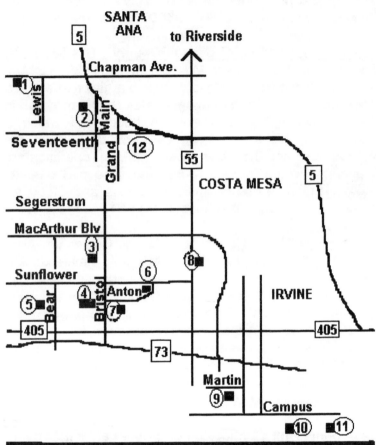

1. Crystal Cathedral
2. Bowers Museum
3. South Coast Plaza Village
4. South Coast Plaza
5. Crystal Court
6. Orange Cnty Perform Arts
7. Sculpture Garden
8. John Wayne Airport
9. Irvine Museum
10. Irvine Barkley Theatre
11. U. C. Irvine
12. Santa Ana Zoo

MAP NOT TO SCALE

DANA POINT AND SAN JUAN CAPISTRANO

Dana Point is named for an early California sailor, Richard Henry Dana, who lent his name to this ocean promontory. His book "**Two Years Before the Mast**" is required reading in all California schools! Dana Point was the major port between San Diego and Santa Barbara and was where the cowhides from the mission at San Juan Capistrano were loaded. Today, it is a picturesque $20-million marina complex that houses 2,500 boats of all shapes and sizes!

To reach Dana Point, we would recommend a leisurely drive down Pacific Coast Hwy. through **Laguna Beach**, past the **Ritz-Carlton Hotel**. This route will afford you some spectacular views of the ocean. As you enter Dana Point, turn right on the Street of the Green Lantern and stop at either **Cannons** or the **Chart House**, two restaurants that overlook the harbor from atop 400-foot cliffs, and which afford a spectacular view and photo opportunity! If you are visiting from January to the end of March you may be lucky enough to see some **California Gray Whales** spouting off the breakwater!

From this vantage point you will get a view of a replica of the **Pilgrim**, a two-masted brig that was anchored in the harbor in 1835, when Richard Henry Dana was a crewman on board. Turn left on Cove Road and follow the road down the steep incline to the **Orange County Marine Institute** (located next to the Pilgrim and the small beach). This is open from 10 a.m.- 4.30 p.m. and there is no admission charge, but they appreciate a donation. Kids love the displays of tidepool life and there is an enormous California gray whale skeleton suspended from the ceiling. There are school workshops planned here regularly, and on weekends visitors can board the Pilgrim. Telephone (714) 496-2274 for information.

In September the Pilgrim is sailed out of the harbor to take part in the **Tall Ships Festival**. The Marine Institute is also the site of the annual **Festival of the Whales**, which takes part in February.

The road along the waterfront is Dana Point Harbor Drive. Continue along this and turn right on Island Way into the parking and picnic areas next to the breakwater, where you can admire the bronze statue erected in memory of **Richard Dana**.

Recross the boat harbor and turn right on Dana Point Harbor Drive to browse through some of the many gift shops in **Mariner's Village** and **Dana Wharf.** They rent boats and skiffs at the **Embarcadero Marina** and offer fishing excursions from **Dana Wharf Sportfishing**. It is great fun to buy a cup of coffee at one of the numerous coffee shops and sit a while watching all the harbor craft leaving or returning to the harbor. This would also be a good spot for lunch.

If you want to enjoy the beach, continue right along Dana Point Harbor Drive and enter **Doheny State Beach** on your right hand side. This is probably Orange County's most popular beach camping spot and it houses a small interpretive center in the park. If you want to just drive through the park to look at the camp sites, the ranger will let you enter for about fifteen minutes free of charge.

After lunch, turn right on Pacific Coast Hwy., and continue to Interstate 5 going north to Los Angeles. Exit at the second off ramp, Ortega Highway/California 74, and turn left over the freeway into **San Juan Capistrano**. You have come to visit the **mission,** located at the corner of the Ortega Highway and Camino Capistrano.

This "**Jewel of the Missions**" is well-known because of the 1940's hit song lauding the annual return of the swallows, but it is also one of the state's most important historical and archaeological treasures. It was begun by **Father Junipero**

Serra, a Franciscan priest,   in 1776 and became a settlement for priests, soldiers and Indians. Today you can tour the mission, which is always under repair, and view the soldiers' barracks, the iron smelter, kitchens and the highlight of the mission, the **Serra Chapel**, the oldest building in California. (Do note the beautiful reredos, an ornately designed gilded wall brought from Barcelona 300 years ago.)

The remains of the **Great Stone Church**, which was toppled by an earthquake in 1812, is still visible and although it has not been rebuilt, there is today a newer Church which serves the parishioners, who send their children to the mission school and attend Church services here.   There is a self-guided tour brochure with a map of the grounds given when you enter. A six-day-long festival that celebrates the return of the swallows is held on March 19 which is called the **Fiesta de las Golondrinas**.

The mission is open daily from 8 a.m. - 5 p.m. in winter and 8 a.m. - 7 p.m. in summer. Admission is Adults $5, senior citizens $4, children ages 3-12 $4, and those under 3, free. Telephone: (714) 248-2048.

Added Attractions in Dana Point

Whale Watching excursions during January through the end of March are offered from Dana Wharf Sportfishing. Telephone (714) 496-5794.

This is a truly awesome experience should you be lucky enough to encounter California Gray Whales on their migration path from their summer feeding waters in the Bering Sea to their breeding lagoons off Baja California.

Added Attractions in San Juan Capistrano.

Los Rios Historic District. There is a walking tour offered every Sunday afternoon at 1 p.m. led by members of the San Juan Capistrano Historical Society. These begin at the courtyard of El Peon Plaza, a cluster of shops across from the Mission. There are also free maps and leaflets available for self-guided tours of the old adobes.
Call (714) 493-8444 for further information.

- Look for the **Rios Adobe** located down the same street, which was built by the local Juaneno Indians in 1794 for Feliciano Rios, who was a Spanish soldier quartered at the mission. His descendants still live in the house.

- Look for the **1894 Sante Fe Railway station** across the train tracks, which is built of handmade bricks. The **Amtrak train** stops here every day on its journey to San Diego. A trip on the train is a fun way to reach this area too.

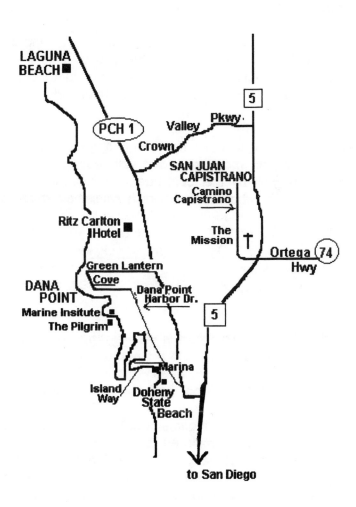

MAP NOT TO SCALE

HUNTINGTON BEACH

There are still a few places where you can spot the remnants of funky, beach life as it used to be in Southern California. This is nowhere more evident than in **Huntington Beach**. Chic modern buildings are side by side with surfing shacks and the hippie lifestyle and the blend makes for an interesting day of touring! The people are equally as eclectic and you can sit and people watch for hours without getting bored!

The main spot to see and be seen is **Main Street**, the two-block stretch of shops and sidewalk eateries that winds inland from PCH. This is where you will see the body builders strutting their stuff, bikers revving their engines and dogs being promenaded amongst scantily and sometimes gaudily clad owners! The area boasts all kinds of spots to eat - our favorite is **The Sugar Shack,** one of the better known sidewalk cafes here. In the evenings this area is very busy with eateries, bars and micro-breweries all jammed to capacity!

At the bottom of Main Street is the **Huntington Beach Pier**. It is almost mandatory to take a stroll to the end of the Pier, of which the locals are justifiably proud! The original pier was built in 1904 of wood, and then replaced in 1914 by concrete (the first of its kind in the U.S.) However, it has been battered by tremendous storms over the years and has now been completely restored to the tune of $10+ million. The city threw a huge party in July 1992 when the work was finally completed on this project, and the pier reopened. There is a **Ruby's Diner** located at the end of the pier.

As you stand at the end of the pier gazing back towards Huntington Beach, the area to the left is the **Bolsa Chica State Beach**. There are many concrete fire pits built on this beach, and it is a great place to come of an evening for a barbecue. There are no city lights in this area, so your stargazing is clear and uninterrupted! (Prior to the state taking charge, this area was called **Tin Can Beach** because of all the hobos who made the area their home!)

To the right of the pier you will see the 8.5 miles of **Huntington State Beach** that makes Huntington Beach famous! Not only is this a wide, beautiful beach but it is crammed with barbecue pits and edged with a bike path that makes walking, rollerblading, cycling or jogging easy and safe! Most weekends you will find surfing, volleyball or basketball tournaments on the go, so there is always something to watch! RV's with prior reservations are permitted to park overnight on this beach.

If you are more ecologically minded, do visit the **Bolsa Chica Ecological Reserve.** These salt marshes are partially restored and the 500 acres that comprise this area are home to some 200 species of birds which use the area as a temporary respite during their yearly migration patterns. You will see all kinds of interesting birds here at any given time of the year, such as the endangered least tern, finches, ospreys, egrets, black skimmers and peregrine falcons. You will see some of their courtship rituals in April and May. The birds enjoy this area for the food they find here too, as the waters contain more than 50 species of fish, as well as clams, mussels and snails.

Bolsa Chica is divided into two sections, the **Inner Bolsa Bay** and **Outer Bolsa Bay**. There is a 1.5 mile trail that will give you a good overview around the inner bay and sand dunes.

There are signs everywhere that describe the evolution, disappearance and re-emergence of these wetlands.

Parking is easy as there are two areas to park - on the south side of Warner Avenue and PCH or about one mile south of Warner on PCH. Both are clearly signboarded. There is no charge and there are picnic tables and restrooms available in the park. **Please Note: Dogs are not allowed in this area - not even on a leash!**

The other parks worth a visit are situated on Goldenwest Street. The **Huntington Central Park** is divided into two sections spanning Goldenwest Street and as you travel from PCH you will find the **Equestrian Center** on your left, followed by the **Frisbee Beach Disc Golf** area.

If you turn left on Ellis from Goldenwest Street, and then right on Edwards, you will come to a large lake on which is situated **Alice's Breakfast in the Park** restaurant. This is half of the Huntington Central Park. This is open daily from 7 a.m. - 2 p.m. This is a super area for the youngsters as it is equipped with an enormous playground in addition to having lots of "hungry" ducks to feed in the lake!

Returning to Goldenwest, turn left and cross Talbert Avenue and the other half of the park will be visible on your right hand side. This area also houses the **Huntington Beach Central Library.** Here you will find **The Park Bench** - another restaurant but one with a twist! They offer a large area, equipped with water bowls and fresh water, where you can rest Fido, and choose a tidbit such as Hot Diggity Dog or Wrangler Roundup from the **Canine Cuisine** menu! On special occasions, such as a doggie birthday, they offer Poochie Parties complete with appetizer, beverage, entree and dessert for a cost of $3.95 per dog! Of course Fido's owners can enjoy their meals from their own menu too!

In the beginning of October, Huntington Beach holds its annual **Sand Castle Festival**. This is located between the lifeguard headquarters and the pier (PCH and First Street), and anyone can participate in building an unbroken sculpture that can reach up to a mile in length.

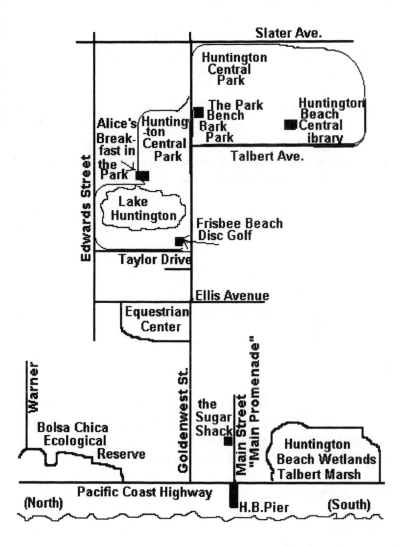

MAP NOT TO SCALE

LAGUNA BEACH AND THE RITZ-CARLTON HOTEL

This is one of the best tours of all - seeing the California coastline at its most charming as well as experiencing the premiere art colony of the area.

We would recommend that you keep on Pacific Coast Highway for the entire day, as this will afford the best ocean views!

Traveling south from Newport Beach towards Laguna Beach is a small area called **Crystal Cove State Park.** This is an unspoiled beach, three miles long, surrounded by forty-five homes - a legacy of early Hollywood film making! There is a little bright yellow shack on the right hand side of the road, called the **Date Shack**, which serves the most marvellous milkshakes, the specialty being the date shake! Sit at their tables and overlook the ocean - it is an unsurpassed view! If you have children with you they will be charmed by the squirrels frolicking in the bushes and underfoot!

Venturing further down into Laguna itself, look out for Crescent Bay Drive on the right hand side of the road, and do a little detour down to **Crescent Bay Point Park**. This is a wonderful little park - lots of weddings take place here, and the view of the coastline is spectacular.

Returning to PCH, take a right on Cliff Drive and follow that through **Diver's Cove** (scuba-diving heaven!) and park just near **Heisler Park.** Parking can be a problem, but try to find a side street so you don't have to feed the meter!

Heisler Park is a great place for a weekend picnic or barbecue in summer, but be sure to get there very early to reserve your spot. Do stop for a moment to watch the lawn bowls - not so common in the U.S.A.!

Your next stop will be **Las Brisas**, a blue and white Mexican restaurant with a pagoda in front of it - another great viewing.

spot and photo opportunity and the site of many, many weddings.

Las Brisas is a excellent restaurant for a special occasion, but it is also fun to sit on the patio admiring the roses and the views of bird rock teeming with pelicans and other marine birds. You may see an artist painting the view from this vantage point!

Continue down the path onto the main beach of Laguna where the annual World Championship Volleyball Tournament is played - always lots of action over the weekends!

Now you are in the heart of **Laguna Beach**. This area has always attracted artists who were inspired by the ocean and the views. A by-product of this is that the village abounds with galleries of every kind. The heart of the village is Forest Ave. and Pacific Coast Highway and you can spend hours in this area admiring the views and shopping to your heart's content! There are excellent restaurants and coffee shops too.

Going up the hill on the other side of the village will bring you to **Laguna Village Art Studios** and shops - this is a fun spot to visit with artists showing their wares and often being available to answer your questions.

The **Hare Krishna center** is close by on Legion Street (a big, pink building) where they have a vegetarian buffet in **Gaurangi's Restaurant** over the weekends - good value for about $6 per person. Also in the area are **The Sherman Gallery** with wacky and funky art, and the **Hotel Laguna** which has a wonderful outside terrace overlooking the ocean!

In the early afternoon, continue down Pacific Coast Highway traveling south until you come to the **Ritz-Carlton Hotel** on the right hand side of the road. This is a very fine hotel and even if you can't afford to stay here, you should definitely take a walk through to see the posh interiors and the lounge that overlooks **Salt Creek Beach Park**. They serve high tea daily between 2 p.m.- 4:30 p.m. The cost ranges from $16.50 for the "Light Tea" on up to $28.50. It is a truly elegant repast. Over weekends there are two seatings - at 2 p.m. and 4:30 p.m. Do call ahead to book if you wish to have tea as it is rather popular - (714) 240-2000.

Christmas time is a good time to visit the Ritz-Carlton Hotel to see the hotel done up in its wonderful holiday decorations. The gardens and flowers are quite lovely, and be sure to go downstairs through the conference centers to the outside walkway overlooking the ocean. Another great photo opportunity!

Additional Notes:

Laguna Beach has three art festivals, all of which are certainly worth while visiting. All three run concurrently from the second week in July through to the end of August.

  a. **Festival of the Arts** and **Pageant of the Masters**. The Pageant presents tableaux vivants - live models posing in the midst of life-size re-creations of famous art.

Each model is in elaborate make up and costume and they appear exactly as their counterparts did in the originals! The Festival of the Arts featuring 100 exhibitors is on display here too. Call (714) 494-1145 for tickets.

  b. **The Sawdust Festival**. This is an outdoor festival of handmade arts and crafts set up in individual booths. There are about 200 exhibitors, who show a wide range of work with many demonstrations of both art and music. Call 494-3030 for further information.

c. **Art-a-Fair.** This Fair features artists who offer classes in painting. The fair sponsors visits by children from the Make-a-Wish foundation and the paintings the children make are sold for charity. There are also art exhibitors here.

MAP NOT TO SCALE

OLD TOWN ORANGE: ANTIQUE LOVERS DELIGHT

The **City of Orange** - **The Plaza City** - dates back to 1869 when two lawyers, Alfred Beck Chapman and Andrew Glassell, accepted 1,395 acres of land from the Rancho Santiago de Santa Ana as legal fees. These lawyers laid out a one square mile town with ten acre farm lots surrounding a 4-acre townsite. Four lots were set aside for the Plaza that throughout the years was to become the symbol of Orange. It is now recorded as a historical site in the National Archives. This community was originally named Richland, but after postal authorities complained, it was changed to Orange.

City lots were originally sold for $6 per acre. Lumber for the houses was hauled in from L.A. and Wilmington. Churches were built and the first public library was established in 1887. By 1900 the population in Orange had doubled with fruit packing and shipping serving as the most important business activities.

Located on Chapman Ave. between the 55 and 57 Fwys. the Plaza City sports hundreds of antique shops, many of them owned by individual collectors who maintain stalls within the larger antique malls. This is the perfect place to find just about anything you ever wanted! These shops are really astounding and all vieing for your attention, so competition is brisk and many a bargain is to be found! There are excellent restaurants in the area, including **Watsons Drug Store and Coffee Shop** just off the Plaza on Chapman Ave. Here you can sit at a lunch counter or in the outdoor patio to watch the passing parade.   They feature handmade shakes and malts and homemade American cuisine!   Amongst the antique shops you will find quaint tea rooms serving a "cuppa" and good pies and cakes!

If you like Cuban food, **Felix Continental Cafe** (right on the circle) is an indoor/outdoor eatery with great food and good prices.

Orange boasts some great fairs every year - an **Annual Street Fair** over the Labor Day Weekend with international food and music as well as many craft stalls, and their new innovation, the **Gogh van Orange** - an art and music festival that they hold in May. These take place right on the circle.

A walking tour (listed below) to see some of the historic homes in the area, all beautifully restored, is a must either before or after you plunge into the antique stores! (The Orange Community Historical Society stresses that these are all private residences and may only be viewed from the outside!)

If you choose not to follow the walking tour, a simple stroll from the center of the Plaza on North Glassell, past Chapman College, and then around the block to Center Street and returning to the Plaza will give you a good idea of some of the restoration that has been done on all these wonderful, old homes. If you are lucky enough, you may see a parrot or two in the trees as they are sometimes to be found in this area!

I. **The Ainsworth House**, 414 E. Chapman Ave. - a museum dedicated to the city's early lifestyle and built in 1910.

2. The 1901 **Finley Home** where Hollywood made "Fallen Angels" in 1945. Go East from the Plaza on Chapman Ave., and turn left on Shaffer Street.

3. **221 N. Orange St**. boasts the oldest documented building in the city and sports a narrow staircase inside. Return along Shaffer to Palm Drive, turn right on Palm Drive and go to Orange St.

4. **Chapman College's** oldest buildings date between 1905 and 1926 and is located at 333 N. Glassell St. (Glassell also runs off the Plaza).

5. On 350 N. Cypress you will find the **Villa Park Orchards Assn. Packing House,** which used to pack more than 80 million pounds of oranges each season. Cypress is located east of Olive.

6. **The Pixley House** build in 1895 is a three-story Victorian mansion located at 288 N. Olive St. Go left past the packing house and turn left on Palm, to the corner of Olive St. and Palm.

7. **O'Hara's Irish Pub** at 150 N. Glassell St. is located in the city's first brick store, circa 1885.

8. **The Edwards House**, built in 1915 is at 350 N. Glassell St., and is where Senator Nelson T. Edwards entertained President Herbert Hoover.

9. 185 S. Center St. houses **St. John's Lutheran Church** - a 1914 building.

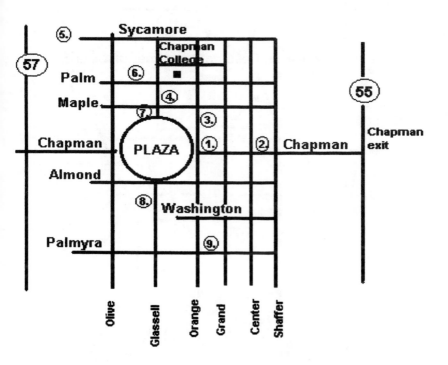

NOTE: Please see map numbers on pages 57 & 58.

MAP NOT TO SCALE

TO THE NORTH: LOS ANGELES AREA

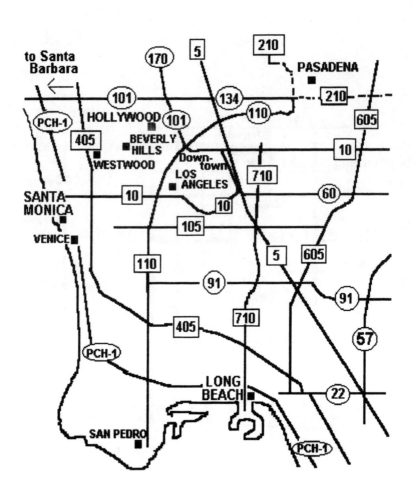

MAP NOT TO SCALE

HOLLYWOOD, BEVERLY HILLS AND BEL AIR

Believe it or not, but **Hollywood** saw its start as a religion-orientated agricultural community in 1903 and became part of Los Angeles in 1910! It didn't take long to become the well-known Movie Capital that we all know and today we find many interesting places to visit!

Travel north on the Interstate 5 to the 10 Fwy. (the Hollywood Freeway) and exit on La Brea. Go north to Wilshire Blvd. and turn left. Continue west for about nine blocks (if you get to Fairfax you will have gone too far!). Here you will find **Rancho La Brea Tar Pits,** a fascinating place to tour as it has yielded more than 4 million specimens of plant and animals since excavation began in 1906. Many of these are from ice-age fossils. These sticky asphalt beds trapped and preserved prehistoric plant and animal life more than 40,000 years ago! You can see the **paleontology laboratory** and view "works in progress" and children can test their strength against the pull of the tar!

Tours of the museum grounds are available Tuesday - Sunday beginning at 1 p.m. The museum is open Tuesday - Saturday 10 a.m. - 5 p.m. Admission is $6 adults, $3.50 seniors and students, $2 children 5-10 years and free for children under 5. **Free admission on the first Tuesday of every month.** Telephone: (213) 857-6311.

When you have finished your tour of the Tar Pits, continue north along Fairfax until you come to Third Street. Time for lunch and what place more fascinating than **Farmer's Market** situated here. This is the original market for the Los Angeles area and boasts more than 150 restaurants, gift shops and stalls of fruits and vegetables. Try some of the more unusual food! The market is located just south of **CBS Television City.**

Continue north on Fairfax a little way until you come to **Melrose Ave.** This area has been made famous by the TV show of the same name. It is set in the middle of an Orthodox Jewish area and is home to the hip and trendy . It is also a good spot for star gazing as many of the big-name studios are located in this area, and Melrose Ave. is where the stars come to play!

Travel further north on Fairfax and turn right on Sunset Blvd. to reach our next stop **- Mann's Chinese Theater.** The hand and footprints of many past and present movie stars are imprinted in concrete in the front of the famous red building and you will have fun finding your favorites! Check out Marilyn Monroe's hands - she must have been very tiny!

After lunch, it is time for a look at the **Stars' Homes!!** Turn left on Sunset Blvd. (west) and then wander through **Beverly Hills** to **Bel Air**. We feel that these are the best homes to see! You will approach a large gate that announces "Bel Air" on the right hand side - drive in and wander up into the hills, gawking as you go at all the magnificent estates! (You may be closely monitored by the local security people - don't let that worry you as they seem to do this routinely). There may be someone in the area selling maps to the star's homes - they put large signs on their cars so you can identify them easily! (Bargain for these and buy them at your own risk - we don't know how accurate they are!)

Additional Places of Interest:

Universal Studios.   We make no mention of this in our text as we assume you will have been there! If not, of course it is a MUST! Telephone: (818) 508-9600. Admission price is $34 adults, $29 seniors over 60 years, $26 children ages 3-11. There will be a L.A. ticket tax added on too!

A fun outing is to visit **Universal City Walk** located near the entrance to Universal Studios. You do not have to pay admission to the Studios to see the City Walk area. This area is full of shops, live performers and restaurants and is a great place to spend some time and have a meal! Validated parking is available.

The Hollywood Bowl. We would be remiss not to mention this famous landmark, and we would heartily endorse an evening spent under the stars at this venue listening to the symphony or another concert of your choice. Pack a picnic basket and enjoy it before the show, or order one delivered to you in your seat. Watch the newspapers for details or call (213) 850-2000 for schedules.

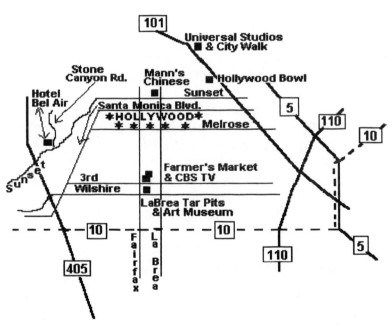

MAP NOT TO SCALE

LONG BEACH, SHORELINE VILLAGE AND THE QUEEN MARY.

Long Beach is California's fifth largest city and is one of the busiest shipping centers on the Pacific Ocean. The city has done a wonderful job in the past several years of revamping the downtown area. It is very pleasant and full of interesting things to do and places to visit!

To begin your day in Long Beach, take Interstate 405 and join the Long Beach Fwy (Interstate 710) to the Queen Mary exit. Continue into the parking lot, for which there is a $7 a day charge. (This is also where the cruises to Catalina Island leave from). Don't forget to get a glimpse of people using the **Mega-Bungee** to the side of the **Queen Mary**!

It is possible to spend the whole day wandering around this magnificent old ship! It was once one of the world's largest ocean liners and crossed the Atlantic 1,001 times before being berthed permanently in Long Beach in 1967.

There are two ways to see the Queen Mary. One is to join a guided tour that will show you areas off limits to the casual stroller, or you may do the self-guided tour, enjoying her decks, cabins and public rooms, all of which are done in Art Deco style. There are enormous photos and exhibits recalling the ship's heyday as a troop carrier during World War II, also as a luxury passenger liner. As an added bonus you will see very cleverly done dioramas showing the hospital, chapel and troop accommodations as well as the gymnasium, children's playroom, beauty salon and dining rooms all set for dinner during happier times! The ship is also renown for bringing over many, many warbrides from England at the close of the War.

Of great interest too, is the engine room with the massive bronze propellers that helped to make this liner one of the fastest afloat in the 1940s. The crew give daily demonstrations with the ropes, lifeboats and engine works.

These days the Queen Mary is run as a hotel, and three decks are reserved exclusively for hotel guests.   There are some very good restaurants on board as well as casual spots for a snack available for visitors.   It is an extremely popular wedding venue! We have also seen movies being filmed here, so keep an eye out for your favorite star! (Bumped into Jack Lemon on our last visit!) You may be lucky!

The entry fee to the Queen Mary is $10.00 per person, seniors 55 and over, $8.00. You will be given a brochure to follow as you do a self-guided tour. There is also a guided tour that costs another $6 which is worthwhile as they show you areas closed to you if you are touring by yourself. These start at 10:30 a.m. and end at 4:30 p.m. and last an hour. The telephone number for further information is (310) 435-3511. Please remember you will get a discount if you show your AAA membership card.

At the base of the ship is the **English Village**, where you can wander around inspecting the shops and stopping for a bite to eat! Do not spend too much time here as the shops are disappointing and don't have much to remind you of England!

This village of thirty shops is quite charming and is nestled next to a boat-filled marina and an aquatic park. If you have children with you, be sure to visit the vintage 1906 carousel. Shoreline Village has many eateries, so take your pick and watch the passing parade as you relax along the water's edge.

There is an excellent **Harbor Spirit Cruise** that gives a 75-minute narrated trip around **Long Beach Harbor** that highlights all the local points of interest, as well as **Whale Watching** trips that leave from the same place during the season. Telephone: (310) 495-5884 for information.

The annual **Long Beach Grand Prix** is also held in the area
below **Wyland's Whaling Wall**. (Check your local newspaper
for dates.)

 Another fun thing to do, if time allows, is to rent a bicycle
next to the parking area and pedal down the cycle path
running along the ocean. There are vendors all along the
shore renting them.

Additional Notes and Places of Interest:

I. There are two historic Spanish homes in Long Beach.
They are **Rancho Los Alamitos** and **Rancho Los Cerritos**,
which have been preserved with their adobe homes and the
original gardens.

To reach **Rancho Los Cerritos** from Shoreline Village,
return north on the Interstate 710 and exit east on Del Amo
Blvd. Turn right on Long Beach Blvd. to San Antonio Drive,
right again to Virginia Ave and then right again to reach
Rancho Los Cerritos. This is open from Wednesday-Sunday
from 1-5 p.m. There is no entrance fee, but they request a
donation. Telephone (310) 570-1755.

This is a handsome two-story ranch house, now a national
historic landmark that was built in 1844 by Jonathan Temple.
Do pay particular note to the gardens he planted more than a
century ago!

Return to Long Beach Blvd., then turn right to the Interstate
405 and follow it south to the Palo Verde Ave. exit. Continue

south on this road past the guard gate to Bixby Hill Road and the **Rancho Los Alamitos** office. There are volunteer guides who will escort you around the ranch house, blacksmith shop, horse barns and dairies. This home was built in 1806 and consists of nineteen rooms. There is a 500-piece collection of American glassware that will be of interest, as will the large gardens. This is also open from 1-5 p.m. on Wednesday-Sunday. Entrance is by donation. Telephone: (310) 431-3541.

2. **San Pedro**, the city north of Long Beach is frequently overlooked, but it too has a very pretty waterfront shopping village called **Seaport Village** complete with restaurants and boat tours and is also well worth a visit. Be sure to check out the fish market where you can order your fish and have it cooked for you outside as you soak up the local ambiance! To reach San Pedro, follow the directions to Long Beach turning off at the Vincent Thomas Bridge. The village is located at the base of this bridge. Cruise ships to Mexico leave from this area.

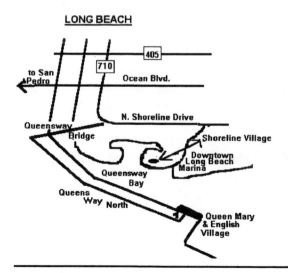

MAP NOT TO SCALE

LOS ANGELES: SHOPPING, SHOPPING, SHOPPING!!

There are growing wholesale districts in **Los Angeles** that lure shoppers with their bargain rates, and we are no exception!

Well known amongst these is **The Cooper Building** at 860 S. Los Angeles Street, where you can browse for fashion bargains. This is Southern California's largest manufacturers' outlet, discount fashion center and covers almost 400,000 square feet on six retail floors. However, in the close proximity between Sixth and Ninth Streets you will find all kinds of garment and jewelry discount stores.

At **Grand Central Market**, 317 S. Broadway, the oldest juice bar in town is a frequent stop of local movers and shakers as well as visitors to the city. This market was opened in 1917 and is the oldest and largest open-air food market in Los Angeles, featuring an array of exotic products such as passion fruit (granadillas), duck eggs, cherimoya, Mexican candies and tomatillos.

The Flower Market, on Wall at Eighth Street, showcases row upon row of fresh-cut flowers and exotic plants. This market is open to the public on Monday, Wednesday and Friday between 8 a.m. - noon, and on Tuesday, Thursday and Saturday, from 6 a.m. - noon.

"The Alley", on Maple Street, is a large area several blocks square selling clothing, jewelry and leather goods very cheaply. It is easily reached from the 405 Fwy.

You may bargain here in some stores, but some will only sell to the trade. Those shops are clearly marked, and it is futile to try to change their minds!

Directions to The Alley: From the 405 Fwy. exit onto the 110 East, then the 10 to San Bernardino. Exit on Maple and continue on until you see some parking garages over the shops on your right hand side (you will see the racks of cloths hanging outside!).   We strongly advise you to park in one of these garages and walk as you cannot drive in "The Alley".   The entrances to "The Alley" are clearly visible. There is, in addition, a large **jewelry mart** in the area at the north end of the clothing shops.

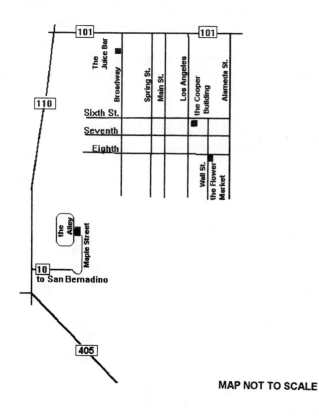

MAP NOT TO SCALE

"MUSEUM ROW" - LOS ANGELES.

In November 1994, Mayor Richard Riordan officially dedicated the eight-block area along Wilshire as "**Museum Row**". This stretch of Wilshire Blvd. between La Brea and Fairfax Avenues was named the **Miracle Mile** more than 25 years ago when it was an active business center.

It has regained its former luster now with the opening of five major museums: **The Petersen Automotive Museum, the Los Angeles County Museum of Art, the Carole and Barry Kaye Museum of Miniatures, the George C. Page Museum of La Brea Discoveries and the Craft and Folk Art Museums**. Plans for this area include a trolley that will connect the museums and Farmer's Market at Third Street and Fairfax Avenue and also landscaping of Wilshire Blvd.

Parking is plentiful in this area and all five museums are within walking distance of each other. All are "child-friendly" too!

I. **THE PETERSEN AUTOMOTIVE MUSEUM**:
6060 Wilshire Blvd.

The exhibits showcase the evolution of the automobile, and also the growth of Los Angeles and the 20th Century. This museum has three floors and the more than 30 detailed exhibits range from a **1911 American Underslung** shown stuck in the mud on a mountain road to a solar-powered car of the future! The second level presents five galleries showing achievements in automotive history. The specialized **Aston Martin** driven by both Sean Connery and Roger Moore in three **James Bond** movies is also on view. There is a special section for two-wheelers and also artworks on the third floor. The museum is open Tuesday-Sunday 10 a.m.-6 p.m.

Admission: $7 adults, $5 students and seniors over 62 years, $3 children 5-12. Parking $4. Tel: (213) 930-2277.

LOS ANGELES COUNTY MUSEUM OF ART:
5905 Wilshire Blvd. Tel: (213) 857-6000.

One of the largest and most prestigious art museums in the country, this museum opened in 1965 with three buildings. It has now grown to accommodate a beautiful sculpture garden, a center for German Expressionist studies, numerous galleries and a pavilion for Japanese art.

The permanent collection ranges from pre-Columbian treasures to the most modern art. It includes such renowned artworks as **David Hockneys "Mulholland Drive"**, the **Gilbert Collection of Monumental Silver** and the **Ardabil Carpet**. Outstanding special exhibitions such as "**Picasso and the Weeping Women**" and "**The Prints of Roy Lichtenstein**" draw residents and visitors alike. There are many film series, art talks, lectures and music performances held here too.

Guided tours of both the permanent and special exhibitions are available Tuesday-Sunday. Open Tuesday-Thursday 10 a.m.-5 p.m., Friday 10 a.m.-9 p.m. and Saturday and Sunday ll a.m.-6 p.m. Admission $6 adults, $4 students and seniors 62 and over, $l children 6-17 years. Free for children under 6. Parking $5, and free after 5 p.m. Closed Mondays. Entrance is free the second Wednesday of every month.

THE CAROLE AND BARRY KAYE MUSEUM OF MINIATURES:
5900 Wilshire Blvd. Telephone: (213) 937-6464.

Carole Kaye's interest in miniatures began in 1990 when she and her grandson built a doll house together! Two years later, when her collection had outgrown her house, she opened the Petite Elite Museum in Century City, and two years ago opened the new renamed museum!

The museum covers two floors filled with miniature houses, figurines, dioramas and objects.

Some of the more intriguing pieces include an antique cloisonné Chinese temple, a Louis XV cylinder desk made of 2,300 inlaid pieces of different woods, and objects such as a complete tea set that sits on a quarter!

Open Tuesday-Sunday 10 a.m.-5 p.m., Sunday II a.m.-5 p.m. Admission: $7.50 adults, $6.50 seniors 60 and over, $5 students ages 12-21, $3 children ages 3-12. Parking will be discounted with a validated admission.

GEORGE C. PAGE MUSEUM OF LA BREA DISCOVERIES:
5801 Wilshire Blvd. Telephone: (213) 936-2230.

This museum is located on the site of the **Rancho La Brea Tar Pits,** one of the world's most famous fossil sites. The Tar Pits have yielded more than 4 million specimens of plants and animals since excavation began in 1906. Many of these - giant ground sloth's, dire wolves, mastodons and saber-tooth cats - are from the Ice Age. These animals became trapped - and preserved - in the sticky tar more than 40,000 years ago! You can see **the paleontology laboratory** where "works in progress" are in full view and you are welcome to observe the fossil preservation and cataloging process. Children can test their strength against the pull of the tar!

Tours of the museum grounds are available Tuesday-Sunday beginning at 1 p.m. The black tar continually bubbles up in the park grounds surrounding the museum. The museum is open Tuesday - Saturday 10 a.m. - 5 p.m. Admission is $6 adults, $3.50 seniors and students, $2 children 5-10 years and free for children under 5. The museum is open Tuesday-Sunday from 10 a.m.-5 p.m. It is closed on Mondays. Free admission on the first Tuesday every month.

CRAFT AND FOLK ART MUSEUM:
5800 Wilshire Blvd.   Telephone: (213) 937-5544.

This Museum was known as **The Egg and the Eye** thirty years ago, but has now undergone several major transformations. **The Egg and the Eye Gallery and Restaurant** opened in 1965 as a resource for unique gifts, ethnic and folk art, books and jewelry. By 1973, interest had been so intense that the Craft and Folk Art Museum was born.

CAFAM's permanent collection comprises more than 3,000 folk art, craft and design objects. It focuses on the folk art of world cultures with a segment on the large Southern Californian populations as well as the work of local craft artists.   It is well known for its **International Festival of Masks**, which takes place each fall.   The Museum Shop stocks unique items such as batiks and ikats from Southeast Asia, Mexican silver jewelry and African beaded necklaces.

Open Tuesday-Sunday 11 a.m. - 5 p.m.   Admission: $4 adults, $2.50 seniors and students and free for children under 12.
Tel: (213) 937-5544.

MORE MUSEUMS - Some of which are mentioned on other tours elsewhere in this book!

1.   Autry Museum of Western Heritage, 4700 Western Heritage Way in Griffith Park-downtown LA. (213) 667-2000.
2.   California Afro-American Museum, 600 State Dr. in Exposition Park-downtown LA.   (213) 744-7432.
3.   California Museum of Science and Industry. 700 State Dr. in Exposition Park-downtown LA.   (213) 744-7400

4.   The Huntington Museum. 1151 Oxford Rd. San Marino (Adjacent to Pasadena). (818) 406-2141
5.   Japanese American National Museum. 369 E. First St. in Little Tokyo.   (213) 625-0414
6.   J. Paul Getty Museum, 17985 Pacific Coast Hwy., Malibu. (310) 458-2003
7.   Museum of Contemporary Art. 250 S. Grand Ave. LA (213) 621-2766.
8.   Museum of Flying. 2772 Donald Douglas Loop North at the Santa Monica Airport. (31) 392-8822.
9.   Museum of Television and Radio, 465 N. Beverly Dr. Beverly Hills. (310)786-1000.
10. Museum of Tolerance. 9786 W. Pico Blvd. West LA (310) 553-8403.
11. Natural History Museum. 900 Exposition Blvd. in Exposition Park. downtown LA (213) 744-DINO.
12. Norton Simon Museum. 411 W. Colorado Blvd. Pasadena. (818) 449-6840.
13. Pacific Asia Museum, 46 N. Los Robles Ave., Pasadena. (818) 449-2742.
14. Santa Monica Museum of Art. 2437 Main St. Santa Monica. (310) 399-0433.
15. Skirball Cultural Center, 2701 N. Sepulveda Blvd. at Mulholland Dr. LA   (310)440-4500
16. Southwest Museum, 234 Museum Dr. on Mt. Washington, LA (213) 221-2164
17. UCLA/Armand Hammer Museum of Art and Cultural Center, 10899 Wilshire Blvd., Westwood. (310) 443-7000.
18. UCLA Fowler Museum of Cultural History, 405 N. Hilgard Ave., West Los Angeles. (310) 825-4361.

PLEASE CALL THE MUSEUMS FOR DIRECTIONS AND INQUIRIES.

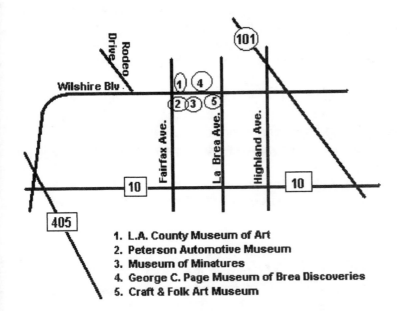

1. L.A. County Museum of Art
2. Peterson Automotive Museum
3. Museum of Minatures
4. George C. Page Museum of Brea Discoveries
5. Craft & Folk Art Museum

MAP NOT TO SCALE

LOS ANGELES. UNION STATION, OLVERA STREET, CHINATOWN AND LITTLE TOKYO

Los Angeles is California's largest city. It was first visited in 1769 by a Spanish expedition in search of Monterey. In 1781 Governor Felipe de Neve and eleven families founded El Pueblo de Nuestra Senora la Reina de Los Angeles (the Village of our Lady the Queen of the Angels). It was the last place to surrender to the U.S. in the Mexican War in 1847. Today it is a bustling area with plenty to see and do!

Union Station on Alameda Street is an imposing white mission-style structure dating back to 1939 and it was one of the last grand train stations to be built in the U.S.A. before air travel became the popular and more acceptable mode of transport.
It is an interesting building to see and of course, the easiest way to get to Los Angeles from Orange County aboard the **Amtrak Train**.

One of the joys of Los Angeles is visiting all the ethnic areas and of these **Olvera Street** is the exact place Los Angeles was born. It was revitalized in 1930 as a Mexican Marketplace and is a good place to buy leather goods (you can still sometimes strike a good bargain, but it is not as easy as it used to be!) and enjoy wonderful, authentic Mexican fare whilst being serenaded by a Mariachi band! Be aware of the potent Margueritas!

Many of the buildings are of historic significance and a visit to the **Avila Adobe**, built in 1818 is a must. There is no charge to enter. It is a self-guided tour and shows the California lifestyle of the 1840s. At the end of the tour is an area showing how the **California aquaduct** was built.

Also of interest is the wonderful **Nuestra Senora de Reina de Los Angeles Church** on N. Main St. at the Plaza, which was completed by the Franciscans in 1822 and is the oldest

Church in the city. Do walk around there a little as there are side chapels outside as well as inside.

The old **Plaza** was the center of activity in the old pueblo and contains a century-old fig tree. The blessing of the animals is held there every year. Do remember to look at all the exotic flowering bougainvillea pouring from almost every crevice during the Summer!

Travel north on Alameda Street until you come to Spring St. Turn right and this will bring you into the heart of **Chinatown,** bordered by Alpine, Spring and Yale Streets. Chinese shops and restaurants provide a look at another ethnic group and you may be lucky enough to see a colorful festival or parade in this area. Great food all over, including, strangely enough, **Little Joe's** - a very old, rather posh Italian restaurant! (This is a super place to eat before attending a show at the Music Center nearby.)   Note: If you happen to be in Chinatown in January, you can see the **Chinese New Year Celebration** and enjoy the **Golden Dragon Parade**.   Of course the shopping is great too - embroidered kimonos, Chinese slippers, toys, jewelry and china as well as fine silks, inlaid furniture and Asian artworks.

Very close by you will find **Little Tokyo**, located between First, Alameda, 3rd and Los Angeles Streets. This is the center for the Japanese community in Los Angeles and also contains many shops and restaurants designed around a rural native village. There are many parades in the area - watch the local newspapers!

This is a good place to get a massage if you have time to do so!   Across the street, **Noguchi Plaza** includes the fan-shaped **Japan America Theater**, which features musical and theatrical performances and a beautifully landscaped Japanese garden.

The **Japanese American National Museum**, located at 369 E. lst Street, is a cultural center illustrating the history of Japanese immigration to the U.S.A. A permanent exhibit depicts the World War II encampments and includes an interactive display that allows relatives to see whether their Japanese ancestors were stationed in the camps.

The museum is open Tuesday and Wednesdays from 10 a.m.-5 p.m., Thursday from 10 a.m.-8p.m. and Fridays, Saturdays and Sundays from 10 a.m.-5 p.m. Admission is $4 adults, students 6-17 years $3, students 18 or older with I.D. and seniors $3, and under 5 years, free. Telephone: (213) 625-0414.

Directions to downtown Los Angeles from Orange County:

Take the I-5 north and then follow the 101 to downtown Los Angeles. Exit on your right on Alameda Street. This will bring you to Union Station on your right and Olvera Street on your left. There are many parking lots in the area ranging from $3-5 per day.

Other Places of Interest in the Immediate Area:

1.   **The Bunker Hill business district** situated near the Music Center, has the **Bunker Hill Spanish Steps**, surrounding the 73-story **First Interstate World Center**, which run from Fifth Street up to Hope Street.

The steps connect the city's hotel district with the **Museum of Contemporary Art** (North of California Plaza at 300 Grand Ave.), which houses a cast collection of Pop Art, modern photography and sculpture. Telephone: (213) 626-6222. (See the chapter entitled Los Angeles: "Museum Row")

This museum, designed by **Arata Isozaki**, a Japanese architect, is a unique work of art in itself, shaped by pyramids, a cylinder and cubic forms. The **Watercourt,** a multilevel landscaped plaza, is located at nearby **California Plaza** and is used for concert programs and community events. It has picturesque waterfalls, an amphitheater and a performing arts space. As part of the **California Plaza** development, the historic **Angel's Flight** has been renovated and reopened. This is the "shortest railway in the world" and it was originally built at the turn of the century.

2. Exiting the 101 Fwy. on Grand will bring you to the **Music Center** - the **Dorothy Chandler Pavilion** (home of the Academy Awards), the **Mark Taper Forum** and the **Ahmanson Theatre**. They also offer tours, and of course the Symphony and theater productions are superb. You need reservations to see most shows, but sometimes you can get "rush" tickets. (Call 1-213-972-7211). Be sure to visit the centerpiece fountain entitled "**Peace on Earth**" - an impressive computer-generated fantasy that will have you enthralled!

3. **The Central Library** reopened at 630 W. Fifth Street following extensive renovation. The main library offers reference services, story hours for children and various programs in addition to books and magazines.

4. Rising from the heart of downtown Los Angeles, near the intersection of Sixth and Hill streets, is a 10-story purple bell tower ringed by hot pink columns, terra cotta spheres and a gold earthquake fault.

The bell tower stands as the centerpiece for the newly re-dedicated **Pershing Square**, the largest and oldest park in the central area of Los Angeles.

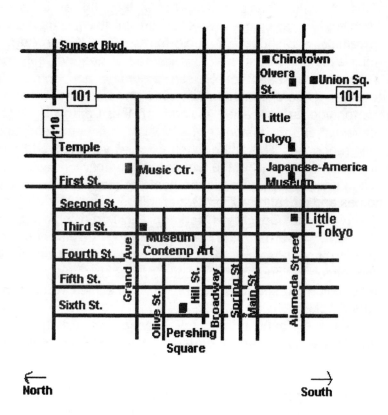

MAP NOT TO SCALE

PASADENA

Pasadena was named "Crown of the Valley" by the Chippewa Indians. It is nestled in the foot of the **San Gabriel Mountains** and has become world famous for its annual New Year's Day **Tournament of Roses Parade and the Rose Bowl Game.** (Please see more information on this at the end of this section). There is lots to see and do in this gracious city, so come with us as we explore!

Our favorite area is the **Mission West Historical District** . This is the image of small-town America with its secluded bungalow homes and shady, tree-lined streets. The area is rich in antique shops and is the home of many fine historical homes and museums. The best are:

The Norton Simon Museum located at 411 W. Colorado Blvd. This museum houses seven centuries of European art from the Renaissance to the 20th Century, and displays works by **Monet, Goya, Degas, Matisse, Raphael, Picasso, Rubens, Rembrandt, Van Gogh, Manet and Renoir.**

The museum is open Thursday to Sunday from noon to 6 p.m. Entrance is $4 for adults, $2 for seniors over 62, $2 for students with I.D. There is no charge for children under 12. Call (818) 449-6840 for further information.

The Huntington Library, Museum and Botanical Gardens at 1151 Oxford Road, San Marino.

San Marino, a close, adjacent city to Pasadena, is one of the wealthiest areas around, so The Huntington Museum is located in a pristine, well-tended neighborhood of large, gracious homes and beautiful gardens. It is always a joy to drive around this area. It is easily reached via either the 110 Fwy. or the 210 Fwy.

The museum itself is superb - a treasury of rare books and manuscripts, furniture, silver, British and French 18th century art, all set among 15 different gardens on grounds that cover 150 acres. The most acclaimed is the **Desert Garden**, the largest mature cacti garden in America, but the most beautiful is surely their stunning rose garden!

A trip to this museum will be a whole day in and of itself if you spend a little time in the beautiful neighborhood too!

The museum is open Tuesdays - Sundays and is closed Mondays. The times are 10.30 a.m. - 4 p.m. Entrance is $7.50 for adults, $6 for Seniors, $4 for students and free for children under 12 years. There is free admission on the first Thursday of every month.   Call (818) 405-2141 for further information.

The Fenyes Estate at 470 W. Walnut St. is interesting as you can see life as it was on "Millionaire's Row" at the turn of the century. It is open on Thursday-Sunday from 1-4 p.m. with guided tours, except for the month of August. Call (818) 577-1660 for more information. Admission is $4 adults, $3 children under 12 and seniors.

The Gamble House was built in 1908 as a home for David and Mary Gamble. This home is internationally recognized as a masterpiece of the turn-of-the-Century Arts and Crafts Movement. It is located at #4 Westmoreland Place. It is open Thursday-Sunday from noon to 3 p.m. Admission is $5 adults, $4 seniors, $3 students with I.D. Call (818) 793-3334 for information.

Other Attractions in the Area.

South Lake Avenue which is Pasadena's business and shopping district located along South Lake Avenue between California and Colorado Blvds.

The Kidspace Museum at 390 S. El Molino, one block west of South Lake Avenue, is loaded with interactive exhibits geared for children under 12 years of age. They have family nights, and also host children's birthday parties.

It is open on Wednesday from 1-5 p.m., Saturday 10 a.m.-5 p.m. and Sunday from 1 p.m.-5 p.m. The last Monday of the month is free from 5-8 p.m. Admission is $5 adults, $5 children 3 yrs. and up, $2.50 for children 1-2 yrs. and seniors and children younger than a year are $1. Telephone: (818) 449-9143.

There is also the **Pacific Asia Museum** at 46 N. Los Robles Ave. which is easy to find as it has an impressive Chinese Palace facade. This museum contains a contemporary Asian arts gallery and a lovely Chinese courtyard garden. It is open Wed.-Sun. from 10 a.m.-5 p.m. The entrance fee is $4 for adults, and $2 for students and seniors (with I.D.) Call (818) 449-2742 for information.

2. Old Pasadena is the trendy area covering twelve square blocks, and is situated inside Arroyo Parkway, Pasadena Ave., Union and Green Streets. This is a quaint and artsy shopping and eating area.

3. The Tournament of Roses Parade is held every New Year's Day along Colorado Blvd. and is one of the finest festivals around, in our opinion! Float after beautiful float, animated and all made of natural flowers, seeds and grasses pass before your eyes as you ooh and aah at them! They are interspersed with marching bands, horses of every hue and size, the two rival football teams who will battle it out later that day in the stadium for the PAC 10 Championship, and many celebrities and city officials. The people around you are worth watching too as many of them sleep overnight on the pavements or arrive the next morning with ladders, chairs and all their paraphernalia! It is a wonderful excursion and well worth getting up early to do!

You will see this written up in the local newspapers for weeks before the great day, and you can pre-purchase tickets to sit in a grandstand/take a bus tour/join various tours, but our best tip is simply to get up at about 5.30 a.m. (depending on your New Year's Eve celebration!!) and drive to the end of the parade route, find a spot and watch them come by! It is hard to miss as they direct the traffic from the 210 Fwy. The floats can also be viewed the day after the parade in Victory Park on 2575 Paloma Street.

Directions to Pasadena from Orange County:

North on Hwy. 57 to the 210 Fwy. to Los Angeles. Exit on Colorado Blvd.

Directions to Pasadena from Los Angeles County:

North on Hwy. 110 and then east on the 210 Fwy. exiting on Colorado Blvd.

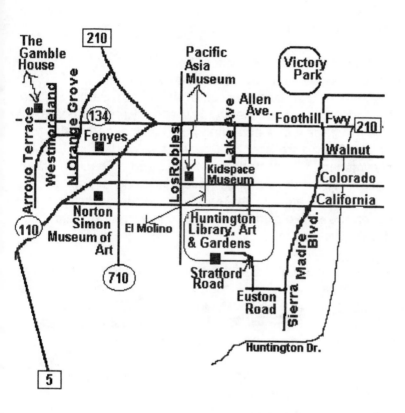

MAP NOT TO SCALE

SANTA BARBARA.

Santa Barbara rests on a narrow shelf between the Santa Ynez Mountains and the Pacific Coast, and is one of Southern California's foremost vacation spots and home to Presidents and lots of polo ponies! This is understandable as you would go far to find a more enchanting area.

Santa Barbara traces its history back to the earliest days of Spanish settlement in California. In 1602, Spanish conquistador Sebastian Vizcaino sailed into Santa Barbara Bay and named it for the saint who held that birthdate. A military fortress was established in 1782 and the mission was founded four years later. Its heritage is evident in its many whitewashed, tile-roofed buildings and Spanish street names. Extensive plantings have made the city a veritable garden and added to its picturesque location and Mediterranean-like climate, you will understand the attraction of this lovely city!

We are fortunate that Santa Barbara is not too far from L.A. and that we can easily reach it in two hours or less, depending on the time of day and the traffic! The route from L.A. along the 405 Fwy. to U.S. 101 is a particularly scenic one and affords many photo opportunities.

Follow signs to **Palm Park** and exit the freeway. This is a popular gathering spot along the oceanfront and on a Sunday is the site of a year-round arts and crafts show. There are many artists living in this beautiful area, so you will see paintings, graphics, photographs, crafts and drawings in abundance.

As you make your way up to **State Street** (the central street and hub of the city) you will find a boardwalk jutting into the ocean - you pay a small fee to enter here, but the views of ocean and mountains are well worth the price!

This is **Stearns Wharf.** You can pick up a snack at one of the stands here, but watch those seagulls who will snatch the food right off your plate! Take a walk up or down the beachfront or travel in style by renting a bicycle from one of the numerous stands in the area.

You will also find the **Sea Center** on Stearns Wharf, which is a branch of the Museum of Natural History. They have some live specimens in saltwater tanks and also display some of the diverse marine life that inhabit the Santa Barbara Channel.

Make your way up **State Street** and enjoy lunch at one of the many eateries in the area. Be sure to sample some of the local area wine! One of the best views of Santa Barbara from all sides is from the top of the **County Courthouse** on Anacapa Street. This has been called America's most beautiful public building. The people in Santa Barbara funded this Spanish-Moorish structure in the 1920's to the tune of $1.5 million. Take the elevator to the bell tower and see the whole world at your feet!

The other must is the **Santa Barbara Mission** located at E. Olivas and Laguna Streets. This mission is called the "**Queen of the Missions**" and was established in 1786. It is one of the best preserved missions in California. (All the missions were created in California to secure the territorial claims in the New World by Spain and under the leadership of Father Junipero Serra twenty-one missions and one assistencia were established, spaced about a day's journey apart.) You can drive to this mission easily from State Street, but if you feel like a bit of a hike, it is a good walk as the homes and buildings up near the mission are beautiful and best appreciated on foot!

There is a mile long **Red Tile Walking Tour** that circles twelve blocks, which showcases many historical, Spanish-style buildings.   Maps are available from the Visitors Information Center at the corner of Cabrillo Blvd. and Santa Barbara Street.

On your return to L.A., be sure to stop in at **Montecito** on the eastern edge of Santa Barbara. (Follow signs from Hwy. 101 - it is one or two exits beyond State Street.)   Exit south on Olive Mill Road, follow it down to Channel Drive on the ocean and have a quick tour of the **Four Seasons Biltmore.**

This 1920's hotel is surrounded by lush landscaping, and is one of California's most elegant beachfront resorts.   The shopping in Montecito is fabulous too!

You should probably make this a lazy day and leave this area a little later than usual to avoid the traffic!   If you choose to visit Santa Barbara for an extended period of time, we suggest the following trip:

l. **Solvang** near Buellton. This village is just north of Santa Barbara and is the closest thing to a Danish village you will ever see!   Windmills and good-luck storks decorate the landscape and they all embody Danish farm-style architecture of brick masonry walls crisscrossed with wooden beams.   The Danish bread and pastries are wonderful!   Do tour the town aboard the Honen, a streetcar pulled by Belgian horses, for a 25-minute narrated tour. (Copenhagen Drive at Alisal Road. Adults $2, children under 12 $1.)

There is also a wonderful open-air theater here (**Solvang Theaterfest**), which is a summer-long repertory theater. Box office is at 420 Second Street.

2. **The Channel Islands** are located off-shore from Santa Barbara. The Parks Board is very strict about these

islands, but they are home to lots of marine life and there are many trips available - overnighters, kayaking, etc. Find out about this on Stearns Wharf.

3. **Ojai**. (Pronounced O-High). This is a secluded valley, 750 feet high in the mountains at the edge of **Los Padres National Forest** in Ventura County, and very easy to reach on your way to or from Santa Barbara. (Travel on U.S. 101 to Ventura, then continue north on California 33 to join California 150 East). Ojai is full of wonderful restaurants and gifts shops and the views to and from the village are stunning. Be sure to go west on California 150 a few miles to see **Lake Casitas**, a man-made reservoir that is a great fishing spot! Rental boats are available here.

Ojai hosts the **Ojai Music Festival** in late May or early June that is an acclaimed weekend concert series held regularly since 1947.

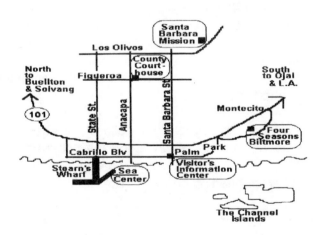

SANTA MONICA AND VENICE BEACH

Santa Monica is a beautiful and picturesque seaside community where the arts and creativity flourish side by side.

To reach this area, follow the 405 Fwy., exit on Interstate 10 south and follow the signs to Santa Monica. The road will drop you off on Ocean Avenue near the **Santa Monica Pier**. This pier is an historical landmark which was built in 1908 and now also includes **Pacific Park**, a family amusement park with roller coasters, Ferris wheels and bumper cars. We would recommend that you park your car in one of the lots available here, and just walk the area as it is quite compact and easy to reach.

This is also a good place to rent bikes and take a spin down the **Pacific Coast Bicentennial Bike Route** that runs along the city's coastline.

Palisades Park runs along the cliffs overlooking the ocean. A walk along the path affords some good views of the ocean and the neighboring area of Malibu. Continue to walk up **The Third Street Promenade**, which is open to pedestrian traffic only. This area is very lively both during the day and in the evening, and you will see live entertainment on the walkway. There is an eclectic range of shops in this area as well as vendors who stroll up and down selling their wares! It is an entertaining area and a must-see!

If you wish to shop, the following areas are ones we recommend, or else simply enjoy the ocean front area with all the eateries and **British pubs**, where you may want to stop for lunch before heading off for Venice Beach.

Santa Monica Place begins at Third and Broadway and is a contemporary retail area full of creative and artsy shops, as well as to some of the bigger department stores.

Main Street stretches several blocks between Pico Blvd. and Marine Street.

The area has been revitalized and rebuilt in the past five years, and you can find retro-style clothing boutiques here alongside thrift stores and museums and galleries. There are also graphic murals decorating the buildings and the walls of overpasses. **The Santa Monica Museum of Art**, in the Edgemar complex on Main Street, displays both modern and contemporary art.

Montana Avenue between Seventh and 17th Streets, is the classiest, most chic area to do your shopping. At its center is the **Santa Monica Antique Market** at 1607 Lincoln Blvd. which houses more than 150 dealers.

VENICE BEACH lies south of Santa Monica between Rose Ave. and Pacific Street. It is best to pay $5 to park in a secured lot and then walk to the beach.

We recommend that you see Venice Beach in the afternoon as many of the street entertainers only seem to appear around noon! It is best to see the sights on a Saturday or Sunday afternoon, but be warned - it is CROWDED! You can spend the whole afternoon wandering around gawking at the local color and watching all the fascinating antics of the street entertainers, not to mention the bodies beautiful all working out at **Muscle Beach** near 18th Street!

Although Venice appears to be a throw-back to the Sixties, it is quite historic and was founded in 1905 by **Abbott Kinney**, who dreamt of building a center for the performing arts and educational activities set amongst a network of canals reminiscent of Venice, Italy. Kinney completed all the canals and then imported gondoliers from Europe to attract visitors and residents to the area. Some of this area is still to be seen if you drive across the four arched bridges on Dell Street. (Call (310) 827-2366 for information about their tours.)

There are some excellent restaurants in Venice Beach such as the **Sidewalk Cafe** where you can sit and people watch.

Other Attractions in the Area.

J. Paul Getty Museum. This is located at 17985 Pacific Coast Hwy. in Malibu, a little north of Santa Monica. It houses one of the world's most valuable art collections in a replica of a Roman Pompeiian villa. The gardens are splendid and the museum a delight. Entrance is free, but reservations are a must in order to park your car. Call (310) 458-2003 a couple of weeks before you intend to visit the museum to secure your parking and entrance. The museum is open Tuesday-Sundays from 10 a.m.-5 p.m. and is closed on Mondays. **Walk-in visits are prohibited**.

** Note: The J. Paul Getty Museum will be moving to its new home within the following year, so please check on location before you go!

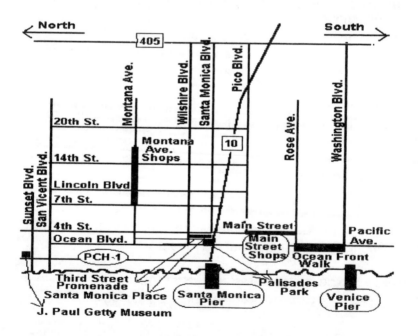

WESTWOOD AND BEVERLY HILLS.

Today you will visit a few of the places that make Los Angeles and the surrounding areas legendary - full of character and charm, and with a good dose of glamour thrown into the bargain too!

Travel on the 405 Freeway, and then exit on Wilshire Blvd., make a left on Sepulveda and this will bring you into the heart of Westwood. **Westwood** is the home of the **UCLA campus**, but the village is worthy of a visit even if you don't plan to see the College. It is a blend of eclectic shops, coffee houses and of course, the super **UCLA at the Armand Hammer Museum of Art and Cultural Center,** located at 10899 Wilshire Blvd. (Tel. (310) 443-7000).

This museum is open Tuesdays, Wednesdays, Fridays and Saturdays from 11 a.m.-7 p.m., Thursdays 11 a.m.-9 p.m. and Sundays 11 a.m.-5 p.m. It is closed on Mondays. The admission cost is $4.50 for adults, $3 for seniors over 65, and $1 for UCLA students. Children under 17 are free. The museum is open for free on Thursdays between 6-9 p.m. There is an additional charge for parking on the grounds of the museum.

As you continue along Wilshire Blvd. you will find yourself in an area of many high-rise buildings - lots of corporate head offices and many Consulate offices are housed in this area. At the corner of Santa Monica Blvd.and Avenue of the Stars you will find **Century City Shopping Center and Marketplace**, a sophisticated retail complex. There are more than 140 stores here and a 14-screen movie theatre plus many restaurants. Century City is also home to **Twentieth-Century Fox Studios**. The magnificent **Shubert Theater** is located here amidst soaring fountains.

Of course, your ultimate destination today is the world-famous **Rodeo Drive** - a shopper's paradise! Do park your car in one of the city's designated parking lots and visit the

"Golden Triangle" on foot! This is the area bordered by Crescent Drive, Wilshire and Little Santa Monica Blvd.

Here you will find **Giorgio Armani**, **Valentino**, **Yves Saint Laurent**, **Bernini**, **Gucci**, **Adrienne Vittadini**, **Bijan**, **Hermes**, **Louis Vuitton**, **Versace** and **Christian Dior** to name but a few! **Harry Winston**, **Tiffany and Co**, **Cartier** and **Cleef and Arpels** sell the most fabulous jewels to the stars and residents of this wealthy community.

We recommend a visit to **Fred Hayman Beverly Hills** where you can relax as you sip a complimentary glass of wine and browse through their merchandise. **Two Rodeo Drive** is one of the most expensive shopping centers ever built where you can be pampered in such salons as **Jose Eber, Aida Thibiant, Georgette Klinger, Tova and Bruno and Soonie.**

Overlooking the whole area is the **Regent Beverly Wilshire Hotel** at 9500 Wilshire Blvd. (where Warren Beatty lived in the penthouse for eight years, and where "Indecent Proposal" was filmed). It is well worth a peek inside to see the lush interior. At Christmas time they have an evening where they turn on the Christmas tree and all the lights of Rodeo Drive, accompanied by children's choirs and your favorite celebrities! (Watch the newspapers for details). All the action happens from the balcony of the hotel.

The Beverly Hills Trolley, reminiscent of a San Francisco-style cable car, takes visitors on a fascinating 40-minute guided tour of the city's historical landmarks and sprawling mansions. Tours run every hour Tuesday through Saturday, beginning at 10:30 a.m. - 5:30 p.m. and the cost is $2 per person, under 12 years free. The trolley departs from the corner of Dayton Way and Rodeo Drive, in front of **Fred Haymans**. This is a most worthwhile tour!

You can also tour the area on foot following a map offered by the **Beverly Hills Historical Society**.   This will take approximately two hours and covers twenty blocks.   Call (800) 345-2210 or (310) 271-8174 for a brochure or stop in at 239 South Beverly Blvd. to pick up copy.

Additional Places of Interest in the Area:

I. **Greystone Park and Mansion**, 905 Loma Vista Drive, has been the site of many movies including "The Bodyguard" and "Indecent Proposal". You may tour the beautiful grounds, but the 55-room house is not open for tours.   Call (310) 550-4796 for information.

2. **The Virginia Robinson Gardens**, 1008 Elden Way, was one of the earliest estates in Beverly Hills and covers six acres.   Reservations are required.   Call (310) 276-5367 for information.

The following homes are not open for tours, but are well worth driving by!

3. **The Witch's House,** 516 N. Walden Drive is worth a look-see as it has a distinctive pitched roof and a wooden bridge that crosses a moat. It was used in silent films before being moved to its present site in the 1930's.

4. **The O'Neil House,** 507 N. Rodeo Dr. is an example of Gaudiesque Art Nouveau architecture including mosiac tilework, skylights and art-glass windows.

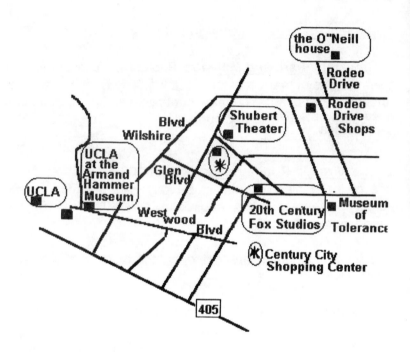

MAP NOT TO SCALE

INLAND AREAS

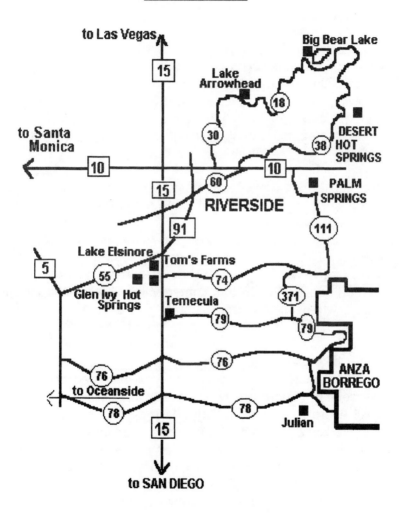

MAP NOT TO SCALE

ANZA-BORREGO DESERT STATE PARK

You may feel as if you are on one of the early roads plunging overland as you venture towards **Anza-Borrego Desert State Park**, and this backroad may well be reminiscent of those roads in the 1800s, but the treasure at the end of it is unsurpassed!

Anza-Borrego is the largest state park in all of the contiguous 48 states and it consists of six hundred thousand acres! It is a sandy landscape studded with a variety of cactus, and following sufficient rain, a profusion of wildflowers. The normal bloom time is early March to the end of April. It is also home to the ocotillo cactus which flowers here in profusion in Spring.

You can become well acquainted with the wildlife, geology and history of the park by following a self-guided nature trail and auto tour. There are special tours led by Park rangers and volunteer naturalists over the weekends in the winter season. There is a visitor's center located in the park containing many exhibits. They also have a nice garden planted outside the visitors center which is fascinating in the Spring when all the cacti bloom! There is a full array of walking, hiking, camping and auto tours in the park.

If you hike the nearby **Borrego Palm Canyon** nature trail, you'll see many more plants than you imagined possible in this setting. There are fifteen desert plants along this path which were used by the **Cahuilla Indians** for food, shelter and medicine. Some of these are creosote bush, honey mesquite, white sage, California fan palms and further along the path a grove of native palms, named in honor of the first U.S. President. The Indians ate the dried fruit and used their fronds to make baskets and footwear. This is a walking tour we would fully recommend as it offers much to see.

Do visit the little community of **Borrego Springs**, a popular retirement community. This retirement oasis is nestled among the majestic mountains. This is the good life - no smog or pollution, freeways or rush hour traffic - just warm sun, pure air and blue skies! The best place for lunch is at **La Casa del Zorro,** and we recommend that you avail yourself of a meal before setting off again for home!

On your return journey, follow the State Road 79 to **Warner Springs** where you may see glider planes soaring up above. These are fascinating as they have no engines and are pulled up by another plane before being cast adrift to continue their journey on the wind currents before landing on the strip right next to the road. There is a $5 day use fee to enter the park. Telephone: (619) 767-5311.

Directions to Anza Borrego Desert State Park:
From Los Angeles: Take the California 60 (Pomona Fwy) east past Riverside and join Interstate 215 and then Interstate 15 south toward San Diego. Just before Temecula, exit east on California 79 to Warner Springs and then turn left on San Diego County Road S2 and into the Park. **From Orange County**: North 91, South on Interstate 15 and follow the above directions.

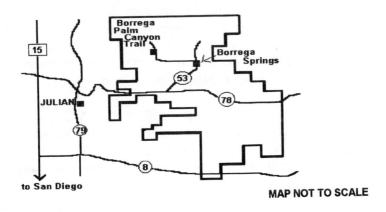

MAP NOT TO SCALE

LAKE ARROWHEAD AND BIG BEAR LAKE

We are so fortunate to have such diverse areas to visit, and the areas of **Lake Arrowhead** and **Big Bear Lake** are within easy distance for a quick day trip. In winter the area turns into a winter wonderland as it is covered in snow, and thousands flock to the slopes near Big Bear. It is equally as beautiful in summer and loaded with places to see and things to do.

The most scenic part of this trip is the area known as **Rim of the World Drive**, which zigzags up the mountainside. Reach it by driving along Interstate 10 (the San Bernardino Fwy), then exit north towards San Bernardino/Barstow on Interstate 215. Follow directions to Highland Ave/Mountain Resorts, California 30, and then take the Crestline/Lake Arrowhead exit, Waterman Avenue. (This is California 18).

You may want to pause at a lookout view site for a good aerial view or to watch the hang gliders as they soar from the mountains to the valleys! Continue along the Rim of the World Drive until you meet California 173 and turn left to Lake Arrowhead.

Lake Arrowhead was rebuilt in 1981 and features some sixty shops and restaurants all situated at the edge of the lake. It is very picturesque and you can board the **Arrowhead Queen**, a paddle-wheeler, to enjoy a 50-minute tour of the man-made lake. You can also rent a motor boat or enjoy some fun in a bumper boat. There are some lovely homes in the area, so you may want to do a short drive around the lake to get a better view of them.

Heading east from the village on California 173, turn left to go west on North Bay Road until it joins California 189 at Blue Jay. This area has a year-round Olympic-size ice skating rink where some Olympians train! Continue south on Daley Canyon Road and rejoin California 18, and then head east again along Rim of the World Drive through **Running**

Springs to **Big Bear Lake**. (This is actually simpler than it sounds!)

You can certainly get sidetracked visiting the **Fantasy Forest at Santa's Village** on your way up the mountain and we would recommend that you do that at another time. It is well sign-boarded and easy to find. (It is open daily from early Nov. thru Jan. 5, at weekends only from mid-June thru mid-Sept. and is closed during March, April and May. The day price is $11, under 2 yrs. free. Tel: (909) 337-2481.) For today however, we would suggest that you continue on, turn right at the dam, follow the road until you reach the Village, and turn left on Pine Knot Ave., which is the heart of Big Bear. The lake is at the bottom of the road and you can spend the whole day shopping on Pine Knot and Village Drive (**Der Weihnachts Markt** is our favorite!) and enjoying the cuisine. There are lots of eateries up and down the street as well as beer gardens, candy-making stores, crafts, etc.

If you are visiting in Winter you need to get up the mountain EARLY to secure your lift tickets for skiing at **Bear Mountain, Snow Forest or Snow Summit** as they sell out early! Night skiing is cheaper and the younger set seem to enjoy it!

There are endless activities - the **Alpine Slide** (winter or summer for the kids), boating on the lake from the different marinas, camping, fishing, golf, hiking, horseback riding, parasailing, tennis and of course all kinds of tours by boat and Jeep. Do remember that it is 6,750 ft. high, so if altitude affects you, do limit your activity! Do drive around the lake to see how large it is! We would also recommend a boat trip on the lake - it is really the only way to view all the homes in the area and all the resorts too!

On the far side of the lake you will see the **Big Bear Solar Observatory**, and across the road from it you may enter the

U.S. Forest Service Campgrounds, from where you can do various hikes up the mountain.

Big Bear is full of cottages to rent for the weekend as well as lots of great Bed and Breakfasts - all of them are easy to find should you wish to come back for a longer time. Do pick up one of the local newspapers found in the village in the newsstands for phone numbers!

Note: This area often experiences icy conditions in Winter and snow chains are often required. These can be rented en route if necessary. The telephone number for the Big Bear Chamber of Commerce is (909) 866-4607.

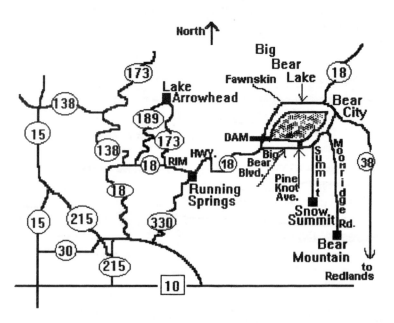

MAP NOT TO SCALE

LAKE ELSINORE, TOM'S FARMS AND GLEN IVY HOT SPRINGS

Since becoming a state recreation park in 1957, **Lake Elsinore** has been a favorite spot for boaters, fishermen and campers.   We go to Lake Elsinore for the other pastime - shopping, shopping, shopping!   The tour we offer today could be a long one, so we suggest you do not linger too long in any one area, or, if you choose to do a lot of shopping, break the tour into two separate days!

To reach Lake Elsinore, travel north on California 91, the Riverside Fwy. and then exit on Interstate 15 at the Lake Elsinore/San Diego sign.   Go south to the California 74/Central Avenue exit and follow the road to the **Lake Elsinore City Recreational Area**. (Tel: (909) 674-3177)

This lake has gone through some changes over the years, even drying up at one point in the 1950's, but it has been refilled with water from the Colorado River and is now a mecca for those in search of tranquillity and water sports! There is a $3 per vehicle entrance fee for day use for two people - extra people are 50c each.   There are boat and bicycle rentals available.

This area used to be known as a health resort, and one of the original spa buildings is still to be seen, the **1887 Crescent Bath House**, commonly referred to as the **Chimes!** The Chimes is now an antique store, but you are still able to view some of the original rooms. The Chimes is 110 years old and a designated historic landmark. It is filled with furniture, glassware, clocks and china in addition to the Roman-style bathtubs, and the massage rooms.

To reach the Chimes, follow California 74/Riverside Drive to Lakeshore Drive and travel east along the waters edge. When you reach the junior high school, bear left onto Graham Avenue in the center of town. Look left for the two-story colonial structure with fancy grillwork on the upper porch.

The Chimes at 201 West Graham Avenue is open weekends only from 10 a.m. - 5 p.m. Saturdays, and on Sundays from ll a.m. - 5 p.m.

Returning to Center Drive, do visit the **Lake Elsinore Outlet Shops**, where a host of well known names offer discounted goods and great bargains! Look for **Liz Claiborne, The Gap, Levi Strauss, Nike, Mikasa, Royal Doulton,** to mention but a few of the stores!

Returning north on Interstate 15, follow signs to **Tom's Farms**, which started as a small roadside stand but which has grown extensively over the years and now comprises several buildings and offers produce, nuts, candies, plants, pottery, baskets, furniture and other goodies. They also have a couple of eateries here, where you can sit and overlook their little man-made lake. We would recommend that you stop here for lunch.

If you have left enough time, do continue to Glen Ivy Road and follow the signs to the **Glen Ivy Recreational Vehicle Resort and Hot Springs Spa.** If you are pressed for time, do pop in and see it for future reference as it is easy to spend a whole day here being pampered and relaxing!

This is one of the oldest outdoor spas around, and is commonly referred to as "**Club Mud**". This resort is a great way to while away the rest of the day and consists of a full-size swimming pool of warm, mineral water along with smaller pools with water coming straight from the hot springs and reaching 104 degrees.

They have shallow lounging pools, wading areas for the children, whirlpool baths and of course the pool filled with red-colored clay that you can pat on to tone up your skin! (Note: Do wear an old swimsuit for this pool as it may get stained!)

In addition, there are private rooms for massages and wraps. You have a choice of shiatsu- or Swedish-style massages, as well as salt rubs and eucalyptus blanket wraps and also facials, manicures and haircuts! You do need an appointment to be pampered, so book ahead to avoid disappointment!

The entrance fee for Glen Ivy Hot Springs is $25 weekends and holidays, $19.50 weekdays, children under the age of 2, free. It is open 10 a.m. - 6 p.m. daily. Call (909) 277-3529 for additional information.

There is a nudist colony called **Glen Eden** situated nearby Glen Ivy Hot Springs. Call (909) 277-4650 if you are interested!

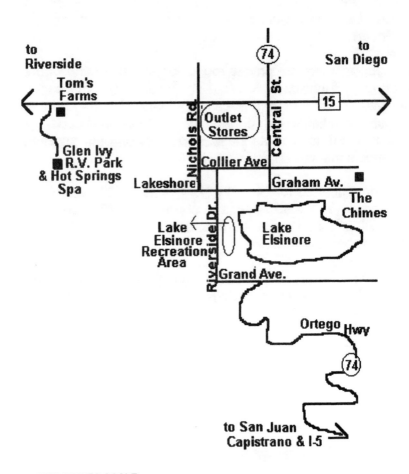

MAP NOT TO SCALE

PALM SPRINGS

You could be forgiven for thinking all the glamour belonged in Beverly Hills, but if you haven't seen **Palm Springs** with its celebrity homes and fabulous resorts, you are in for a surprise!

With about 1,500 palm trees lining its main thoroughfare, Palm Canyon Drive, it is truly well named. There are also hot springs here, dating from when the **Cahuilla Indians** came to relax and find healing powers in their hot mineral waters. Palm Springs is still largely owned by the Agua Caliente band of the Cahuilla Indians and they lease out much of the land to the large resorts, making the 200 tribal members the wealthiest Indians in the nation. They also own the **Casinos** that dot the landscape - yes, gambling is legal on the Indian-owned land!

Palm Springs is truly a year-round playground for everyone and our recommendation is that you orient yourself by taking a guided tour on a **Celebrity Tour** in a smaller bus. This will provide an extensive look at Palm Springs and the adjoining communities, show you many homes belonging to stars, such as **Bob Hope, Elvis Presley, Red Skelton, Debbie Reynolds, Paul Newman, George Burns, Gene Autry, Danny Kaye, Frank Sinatra, Liberace and Lucille Ball**, to mention only a few!

Celebrity Tours, 174 North Indian Avenue, Suite 10, offers two tours as follows: The "A" Tour, which lasts an hour, costs $11 for adults and $10 for Seniors and leaves at 10:15 a.m. and 1:45 p.m. The "B" Tour, which lasts 2 1/2 hours, costs $16 for adults and $14 for seniors. It also leaves twice a day at 8:45 a.m. and 12:15 p.m. Tel: (619) 770-2700.

If you are not star-struck, then rent a bicycle and ride along the 35 miles of bike paths. These are available from Burnett's Bicycle Barn (429 South Sunrise Way at Ramon Road) or Mac's Bike Rental (700 East Palm Canyon Drive).

Of course, there are resorts, hotels, golf courses and pools galore in Palm Springs (7,000 rooms, 600 tennis courts, 70 golf courses and some 7,500 swimming pools!) so you need not be bored in this city! The shops are super, and so are the restaurants.

Another famous attraction is the **Palm Springs Aerial Tramway**, off California 111 via Chino Canyon Road. This Tramway is the longest single-span passenger tramway in the world and it has been open since 1963. You will travel from the desert floor to 8,516 ft. at the mountain station. There is a taped commentary telling you all about it as you ascend. **The Alpine Restaurant** is situated at the top of the mountain. Please Note: It can be quite chilly at the top of the mountain, so dress accordingly.

This is open daily except in early August when they do maintenance. The first cars up are at 8 a.m. weekends, 10 a.m. weekdays and the last car down is at 9:15 p.m. in winter and 10:45 in summer. The cost is $16.95 for adults, and children 3-12 $10.95. Telephone: (619) 325-1391.

NOTE: Do remember to carry a sweater with you as the evenings can turn pretty chilly in the desert. Remember - high season in the desert is during winter, but some great bargains are to be had during the Summer months! All buildings are airconditioned, so you won't suffer too much when the thermometer tops 100 degrees!

Hints to help you sound like a local!

Palm Springs has strict ordinance that forbids flashing, rotating, neon or garish signs, so places such as McDonald's may have a sign, but no golden arches! Building codes prohibit new homes from casting a shadow on neighboring homes!

No accomodation is a "Motel" - the word is banned. They are all called "Hotels" - even the "Hotel 6!"

Directions to Palm Springs from Orange County:

Take Hwy. 91 (the Riverside Freeway) north to the Interstate 10 East. Follow it all the way to California 111 which delivers you into the heart of Palm Springs.

Directions to Palm Springs from Los Angeles County:

Head east on Interstate 10 and join California 111 which delivers you into the heart of Palm Springs.

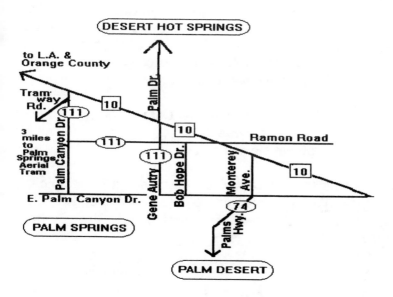

MAP NOT TO SCALE

SANTA CATALINA ISLAND

Located just 26 miles from Orange County, **Catalina Island's** seventy-six square miles are covered with broad valleys, isolated coves, pristine beaches, two thousand foot peaks and near vertical shoreline palisades. It is a wonderful place to escape for a day and offers golfing, deep sea fishing, diving, shopping, dining, ocean rafting, sunbathing, swimming, camping, hiking, biking, kayaking, sailing, parasailing, jet skiing - to mention a few things to do!

Getting there is easy! You can hop aboard the **Catalina Express** from **Long Beach** for an hour's fast trip, but the **Catalina Flyer** also leaves from **Newport Beach** and takes 75 minutes. The cost of the ride is $33 round trip for adults, seniors $30.50 and for kids 3-12 $16.50. There are many different departure and return times from Long Beach, and you will need to reserve your seat on the ferry well in advance by calling (310) 519-1212. The Catalina Flyer from Newport Beach leaves at 9 a.m. every day and leaves Catalina at 4.30 p.m. (Call (714) 673-5245 to make your reservation). In addition, there is a helicopter service offered from Long Beach at the foot of the Queen Mary.

Once in **Avalon** - the only town on Catalina Island - you will have an array of tours available or you can take yourself off for any of the above mentioned pursuits!

We recommend that you at least do a tour through **Discovery Tours**, located in the center of Avalon who offer single or combination tours of the following: **Glass Bottom Boat ($8), Casino Tour ($8), Scenic Tour of Avalon ($8), and the Botanical Gardens Tour ($14.50).** We think the Scenic Tour is a must. In addition, they offer a **Seal Rocks Cruise** for $8 in the summer. All the above are short tours of an hour or less. The longer tours include the **Skyline Tour** (2 hours, $16.50), the **Inland Motor tour** (4 hours, $29) . The latter tour takes you ten miles inland for a scenic look at the island's geography and native plant life. You may see some wild boar and bison up here too! The Skyline Tour takes you up the mountain to the airport and has fabulous views looking down on the island.

The Scenic Tour will show you the whole town - it is only about a mile square - including such highlights as **Zane Grey's Pueblo** (where he wrote many of his books) and the **Wrigley Mansion** (bought by William Wrigley, Jr. of the chewing gum family) and now run as the **Inn on Mt. Ada**. The views are spectacular from the top of the hills winding back intó the town where you will find the **Casino** - long ago home of the big bands where the jet-setters used to visit from the mainland to dance the nights away. Mostly though, it is the views of the harbor and all the boats that are so fascinating. These tours can also be purchased on the boats on the ride to the Island.   Tel: (310) 510-2000.

If you choose to wander around by yourself, there are shops and restaurants aplenty and many quaint inns and Bed and Breakfasts to investigate for future trips! Parts of Avalon are steep, and you may feel more comfortable renting the most popular form of transportation on the island - the golf cart! You can certainly do your own "tour" this way too!

To reach the boat terminal at Long Beach:
Exit from the 405 and follow Interstate 710 south to Long Beach. Follow the signs to the Queen Mary and enter the Queen Mary parking lot and follow the blue line to the left to the Ferry terminal. It will cost you $7 to park for the day.
To reach the Catalina Flyer:
Follow Pacific Coast Hwy. to Jamboree.   Turn right and follow the road, over the bridge onto Balboa Island. Follow signs to the Ferry. Our suggestion is to park on the Balboa Island side (you can park for free on a side street) and then catch the ferry across the harbor to the foot of the Ferris Wheel.   The Catalina Flyer is parked next to the Balboa Pavilion and is easily visible. (Balboa Island map - page 34.)

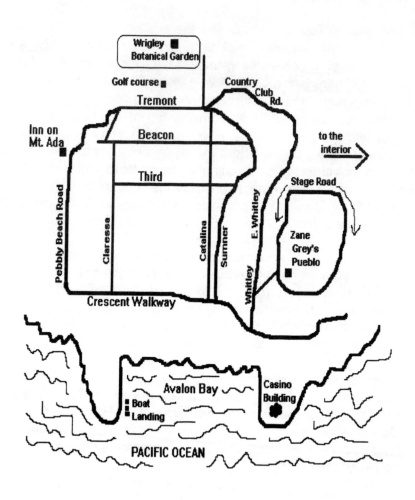

MAP NOT TO SCALE

SOUTH OF THE BORDER:
TIJUANA AND ROSARITA BEACH

Mariachis, Margueritas! Great food and bargains galore! Friendly people and a relaxed atmosphere! All of these are good reasons to spend a day exploring the Mexican towns just south of the border! U.S. citizens do not need a passport to enter **Baja California**, but be sure to bring some photo identification such as a driver's license which they will ask for on your way out. You don't have to change money as American dollars are well accepted in Mexico, and you won't have a language problem as most of the locals speak English!

So, join us as we wander down the Interstate 5 to the U.S.-Mexican border. If you intend to drive into Mexico, we would recommend that you stop to buy Mexican insurance for your car just prior to reaching the border, as U.S. policies are not valid there if you have an accident. (You may also obtain this from your agent.) You will see many signs advertising this! (Note: If you are nervous about driving, you can walk over the border and take a taxi into the main shopping area).

Once over the border, follow the Centro signs to downtown **Tijuana** and drive down the main street, **Ave. Revolucion**. Turn left on Calle 7 (7th Street) and park in the guarded parking lot at the **Fronton Palacio**. This is at the top end of the street and identifiable as the Jai Alai Palace by the statue of the athlete in the front! **Jai Alai** is an ancient Basque ball game. Fun to watch if you can manage to see them playing at 8 p.m. nightly except Thursdays. They have parimutuel betting.

Wander back down Ave. Revolucion bargaining for leather goods (don't be put off by the "marked" prices on the merchandise), especially handbags and belts.

Perfume, vanilla, Kahlua liqueur and Tequila are cheaper here (one quart per adult is allowed duty free by U.S. Customs), silver jewelry (look for the stamp on the back for authenticity and remember that they use a different weight of silver to make their jewelry, but it is all good silver!) and clothing.

We suggest that you eat at **Tijuana Tilley's** or **Pedrins** across the street. You will be safe having water in these restaurants, but **please do not drink unbottled water on the streets of Tijuana or anywhere else in Mexico for that matter! Remember - this applies to ice in your drinks too!** The better class establishments will provide pure water for their patrons. Tijuana Tilley's is located at the base of Fronton Palacio.

As you leave Tijuana, follow the Rosarito/Ensenada Toll Road (Cuota) signs through town to the four-lane highway that leads south to the beach at **Rosarita**, home to many Americans, a lot of them retired! After passing through the first toll station, take the first Rosarita exit and enter the north end of town.

Travel south on Rosarito's main street until you see the arched entrance to the **Rosarito Beach Hotel**, built in the 1920's. This resort is very popular, but was once a hideaway for the rich and famous! There are immense murals and artwork in the hotel, including hand-painted ceiling beams and in the main dining room, framed images of six Aztec gods made out of yarn on a base of beeswax! It is a worthwhile stopping place! Telephone: (619) 498-8230 for reservations.

You will find miles of wide, sandy beach outside the Rosarito Beach Hotel as well as horses to ride should you so wish!

Please note that your return trip could be somewhat arduous as the Mexican-U.S. border is inclined to get jammed up and you could sit there for quite a long time! You will be delighted by the street vendors and all their stalls to enliven your wait!

Additional Places to See:

IN OR AROUND TIJUANA:

1. **Plaza Rio Tijuana**, is a covered complex of over 100 shops situated in the city's reclaimed riverbed. There are many big department stores here as well as a supermarket and a good bakery called **Suzett Bakery and Pastry Shop**. This center is situated a few blocks east from Avenida Revolucion.

TIJUANA AND ROSARITO.

2. The locals are justifiably proud of **The Tijuana Cultural Center**, a huge eight-story sphere which houses an **Omnimax Theater** and museum. They show a panoramic film presentation of "**City of the Sun**", which describes the history of Mexico. This is narrated in English and shows every day at 2 p.m. Very worthwhile! This Center is located on Paseo de Los Heroes and is open from 11 a.m. - 8 p.m. on weekends and to 7 p.m. on weekdays.

3. **Agua Caliente Racetrack**, three miles from downtown is a favorite place for Americans to visit. There are eleven horse races every Saturday and Sunday - Post time is noon. Greyhound racing dogs compete in the same arena when it is not being used for the horses. The dogs race every night at 7:45 p.m. except Tuesdays.

4. **El Toreo Bullring**. Mexican matadors perform here on Sunday afternoons at 4 p.m. from mid-May to mid-July, then at **Plaza Monumental Bullring-by-the-Sea** until October.

ROUND ROSARITO BEACH.

Twelve miles south of Rosarito Beach on the old Ensenada Highway you will reach the fishing village of **Puerto Nuevo**. This is renown for its fresh lobster dinners, and is owned by the Ortega family who operate six restaurants in the area. Your meal will be served with rice, refried beans and flour tortillas. The prices are good - a small lobster will cost about $10, the medium size (about 1-1/4 lbs.) $12, the large size $15 and the huge $19. Look for the entrance to Puerto Nuevo about two miles after **Las Gaviotas** resort development.

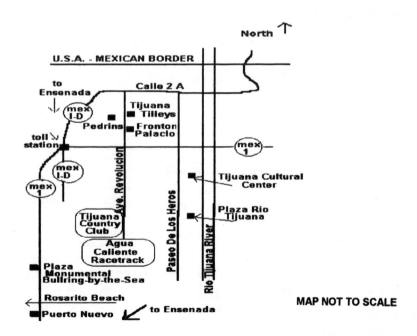